SOCIO-RELIGIOUS ESSAYS ON AMERICAN SOCIETY

SOCIO-RELIGIOUS ESSAYS ON AMERICAN SOCIETY

A creative collection addressing the pressing issues plaguing America's basic primary institutions: family, church, and educational institutions.

BOBBY MILLS, PH.D.

Socio-Religious Essays on American Society
by Bobby Mills, Ph.D.

Cover Design by Atinad Designs.

© Copyright 2015

SAINT PAUL PRESS, DALLAS, TEXAS

First Printing, 2015

ISBN-10: 1517442451
ISBN-13: 978-1517442453

Printed in the U.S.A.

Contents

 # *Acknowledgments*

Americans need to come together in moral-spiritual unity in their homes, churches, and educational institutions always seeking to do the right thing. In my personal and professional life, I have always tried to *think* in intellectual integrity constructs that do not permit my mouth to get in front of my mind. But, more importantly, I have always tried to live by the *fruits of the spirit.*

I thank my family for their loving support during my college teaching career—especially my wife, Larnita; my son, Daryl Anthony; and my daughters, Kelly Leigh and Karen Rene'. Grateful appreciation and heartfelt thanks are extended to Clara M. Bowman for assistance with manuscript formatting. To Charles W. Moore, for our friendship and stimulating spiritual conversations. To Pastor Lewis

C. Parker Jr., Pastor Raymond L. Farley, Pastor John
E. Cameron, Pastor Henry S. McCullum, and Pastor
Clifton Goodloe Jr., for our spiritually based friendships
over the years.

Finally, to Sharon C. Jenkins, for her tireless
professional editing of the manuscript, as well as her
spiritual insights in helping to make America a more
just and loving society.

I love and thank you all. God's choice blessings
to you and yours.

 # *Introduction*

First of all, as Americans, we must find creative socio-spiritual (non-violent) to solve societal ills and resolve issues of social injustice simply because we are morally obligated to live up to the conscience of the spiritual words recorded and agreed to in the Preamble to the U.S. Constitution:

> We hold these truths to be self-evident that all men are created equal, that they are endowed by their Creator with certain inalienable rights, and among these are life, liberty and the pursuit of happiness.

The U.S. Constitution is *almost* a perfectly written governing document. It was a document that the world had never seen before, because it included everyone as equal members of society; not even the Magna Carta included everyone. However, the legal enforcement of the document is mired in race/ethnicity, social class, and gender discrimination.

Second, as a nation, we must help permanent-tan-ethnic minorities understand the nature of cause and effect, that is, the consequences of their own behavior concerning their socio-economic plight. To be sure, the behavior of *some* Whites has been notoriously bad over the past four hundred years. Institutional racism has become a self-fulfilling prophecy primarily because some Whites act as though they are superior and some minorities act as though they are inferior. Therefore, we may not have racism by law, but racism still exists in individual mindsets and institutional power sources.

No human being can do more for an individual than that which an individual can do for himself or herself. The nature of the problems confronting American society is both spiritual as well as sociological. Lack of economic justice is only a symptom of the problem. The real problem is a lack of spiritual unity and economic structural organization.

As an individual thinks, so is he. Despite institutional

arrangements and social barriers that are designed to impede the progress of ethnic minorities toward economic liberation, individuals are spiritually and morally called to overcome such obstacles. Those of us who know better should do better. That is, we should provide ethnic minorities with life-changing behavioral and economic strategies that can transform the socio-political-economic dynamics of ethnic communities. Moreover, those of us who have turned-the-corner have a sacred obligation to look back and reach back, and help minority communities create the ability to supply their own communities with basic, life-sustaining necessities (goods and service). This, in turn, will halt the participation of minorities in their own social, economic, and cultural demise. Too many minorities have become a part of the institutional and cultural dehumanization problem, rather than the solution to the problem.

In the twenty-first century, the moral picture of American society looks bleak, especially in the Black community. Prior to the passage of the 1964 Civil Rights Act and the 1965 Voting Rights Act, Blacks had a more moral, accountable, and trustworthy leadership mentality and a more viable, morally and economically productive community that was controlled internally rather than externally. By and large, the Black leadership mentality was housed in the Black church experience, not in the political arena. Allow me to take you to spiritual higher ground with a sacred Scripture from 1 Peter 2:9-10, because you are God's own people: "But ye are a chosen generation, a royal priesthood, a holy nation, a peculiar people; that ye should show forth the praises of him who have called you out of darkness into his marvelous light: to which in time past were not a people, but are now the people of God: which had not obtained mercy, but now have obtained mercy."

Too many Americans are walking and talking after the flesh and are maximizing the pleasure principle and chasing material things, rather than embracing the spiritual and moral development of the heart and mind. The righteousness of God is not necessarily embodied in civil and criminal law, but all law was fulfilled in the teachings and life of Jesus. After all, Jesus was the greatest teacher to have lived because He was a teacher sent from God.

Seeking to maximize the pleasure principle is a dangerous life proposition. "But she that liveth in pleasure is dead while she liveth" (1 Timothy 5:6). She, in this biblical context, refers to both sexes, females and males alike. Pleasure in this scriptural context is not just a reference about sexuality. Eating for pleasure is extremely dangerous to an individual's well-being. As Americans, we must be honest with each other in our analysis of the nature and condition of life in our country today. And, of course, this is precisely what this book is attempting to do.

- We have too many children being born out-of-wedlock.
- We have too many children having children. (Children becoming mothers and fathers before becoming women and men and wives and husbands is out of moral order.)
- Too many Christian churches with celebrity preachers, rather than godly pastors.
- Too many teachers who "show-up and pick-up" checks rather than love, serve, and teach children.
- Too much societal misinterpretation of second amendment rights, and not enough embracing of first amendment rights: life, liberty, and the pursuit of happiness.

Therefore, we must ask ourselves the question: what happened? The intellectual intent of this book of essays on the problems facing American society is not to blame but to reclaim. That is, to intellectually interpret the socio-spiritual-economic meaning of this state of affairs for the masses. The author is attempting to give Americans a unifying moral choice between life and death, because "to one who knows the right thing to do, and does not do it, to him it is sin" (James 4: 16-17).

The choices are clear: God's blessings or God's curses. After all, freedom is not free because freedom is not birthed out of being irresponsible. It has rightly been said: "To thine own self be true." As an individual thinks, so is he. There is a clarion call blowing in the wind: change direction. Without a doubt, the fervent prayers of the righteous can accomplish much. Selah!

Christian Sustainability, Credibility, and Accountability

1

The Christian church is of divine intent, not a human invention. Even in the midst of our twenty-first century moral confusion and chaos and *some* double-minded, prosperity-preaching pastoral leadership, the church will forever belong to Jesus Christ. As it is spiritually recorded: "And I say unto thee, That thou art Peter, and upon this rock I will build my church; and the gates of hell shall not prevail against it" (Matthew 16:18). Christianity is sustained by the will of God and there will always be some men and women who will be obedient to the Jesus-way, which is God's Word and God's will, because deliverance always comes by the power of God. For after all, the

Christian church is an organism, not an organization.

Sustainability

"There is therefore now no condemnation to them which are in Christ, who walk not after the flesh, but after the Spirit. For the law of the Spirit of life in Christ Jesus hath made me free from the law of sin and death. For what the law could not do, in that it was weak through the flesh, God sending his Son in the likeness of sinful flesh, and for sin, condemned sin in the flesh: that the righteousness of the law might be fulfilled in us, who walk not after the flesh, but after the Spirit" (Romans 8:1-4) This Scripture is the spiritual basis for why the church will always be sustained as part of God's ordained, divine purpose. Likewise, there are profound spiritual questions that every living soul must ask of one's own self. "What! Know ye not that your body is the temple of the Holy Ghost which is in you, which ye have of God, and ye are not your own? For ye are bought with a price: therefore glorify God in your body, and in your spirit, which are God's" (1 Corinthians 6: 19-20). Likewise, "What shall we then say to these things? If God be for us, who can be against us?" (Romans 8:31). To be sure, we must ask God for permission in all things.

Credibility

God has placed before Christians a question of credibility and He has also provided us with a spiritual/ moral answer. This affirmative answer must be a very personal decision for everyone: "I am not ashamed of the gospel of Christ: for it is the power of God unto salvation to everyone that believeth; to the Jew first, and also to the Greek. For therein is the righteousness of God revealed from faith to faith: as it is written, The just shall live by faith" (Romans 1:16-17). And, of course, it is our spiritual/moral obligation to "study to show thyself approved unto God, a workman that needeth not to be ashamed, rightly dividing the word of truth. But shun profane and vain babblings: for they will increase unto more ungodliness" (2 Timothy 2:15-16). Unfortunately, far too many Christian churches are engaged in profane and vain babblings as babes in Christ. But, based on the precepts of the Old Testament, we know what we must do in order to live according to the Will of God: "Blessed is the man that walketh not in the counsel of the ungodly, nor standeth in the way of sinners, nor sitteth in the seat of the scornful. But his delight is in the law of the Lord; and in his law doth he meditate day and night. And he shall be like a tree planted by the rivers of water, that bringeth forth his fruit in his season; his leaf shall not wither; and whatsoever he doth shall prosper. The ungodly are not so: but are like the chaff which the wind driveth away. Therefore the ungodly shall not stand in judgment, nor sinners in the congregation of the righteous. For the Lord knoweth the way of the righteous: but the way of the ungodly shall perish" (Psalm 1:1-6).

I have no reason or intention to condemn Christian churches, just as God does not find condemnation in Christian churches. However, I would merely encourage pastoral leaders to preach the "Good News Gospel." For, without a doubt, the Good News Gospel is God's Gospel. This is why Jesus commissioned the disciples by saying, "Go ye into all the world, and preach the Gospel to every creature. He that believeth and is baptized shall be saved; but he that believeth not shall be damned" (Mark 15:15-16).

Accountability

The Word is God's Word, not the pastor's words. And, of course, "All scripture is given by inspiration of God, and is profitable for doctrine, for reproof, for correction, for instruction in righteousness: that the man of God may be perfect, thoroughly furnished unto all good works" (2 Timothy 3:16-17). This Scripture applies to all Christian believers because all Christian men should be men of God. Pastoral leaders have the spiritual duty to be under-shepherds to the Good Shepherd: Jesus Christ, the righteous one. To be sure, pastoral under-shepherds or laymen, must abide by the following (edited) precept: "For we must all appear before the judgment seat of Christ; that everyone may receive the things done in his body, according to the things he hath done, whether it be good or bad" (2 Corinthians 5: 10).

The demographics of church attendance are vastly different for black and white communities. From a sociological perspective, whites and blacks attend church for different spiritual reasons. Both attend church to thank God for what they have because things could be worse. By and large, whites attend church for reasons of individual conscience and moral redemption, not to change societal conditions because they personally benefit from current societal conditions. White churchgoers are truly the "silent majority" and, of course, this is why eleven o'clock on Sunday morning is the most segregated hour in American society. However, what individuals do and say in the dark will eventually come to the light, whether good or bad. "If we say that we have fellowship with him, and walk in darkness, we lie, and do not the truth: but if we walk in the light, as he is in the light, we have fellowship one with another, and the blood of Jesus Christ his Son cleanseth us from all sin" (1 John 1:6-7).

Far too many whites have not broken the yoke of the mentality that says, "I'm doing fine, and to hell with everybody else; I must protect that which is mine at all costs." Stuck in the mentality of rugged individualism, they forget that everything belongs to God, and we are only stewards of God's bounty. Of course, whites do share with each other based upon the notion of who deserves and who does not deserve. The concepts of white privilege and manifest destiny do not account for the reality and role of free black labor, and likewise, in the twenty-first century, the concept of "cheap labor" has become the overriding spiritual/moral factor in American society. "Righteousness exalteth a nation: but sin is a reproach to any people" (Proverbs 14:34).

Therefore, whites attend church to appease their moral conscience against their inaction, that is, for "saying nothing and doing nothing" in the midst of confusion and more confusion. "For God is not the author of confusion, but of peace, as in all churches of the saints" (1 Corinthians 14:33).

Blacks, on the other hand, attend church beseeching God's benevolent assistance in their deliverance from economic bondage, because they are in "Egypt" with their backs against the "Red Sea," that is, that economic wall of spiritual, moral and social injustice. Because of this wall of institutional racism, far too many blacks have not broken the yoke of a "poor ole me" mentality.

God delivered the Hebrew nation, and of course, God can deliver blacks if they are obedient to God's Word and His will. "And we know that all things work together for good to them that love God, to them who are called according to his purpose" (Romans 8:28). This Scripture is just a little taste of the "pie in the sky," but, oh, how true it rings as America seeks a just society. "But if we hope for that we see not, then do we with patience wait for it" (Romans 8:25).

There may have been no room for Jesus at the inn, but there will always be room for Jesus in the Christian church because the church is not sustained by flesh and blood or perpetuated by brick and mortar, but by God's Word.

An Open Letter to American Pastoral Leaders

2

Pastoral leadership in American society prior to the Civil War never actually took a conscious stand for godly morality, only for geographical regionalism; unfortunately, the same political mentality exists in the twenty-first century. Even today, *some* politicians vehemently declare that systemic racism is a phenomenon of the past. America's military fights for human rights on foreign soil and, at the same time on American soil, our social system violates the civil rights of minorities via the institutions of voting and police accountability. Of course, it is true that there are no racist laws in existence today. But, all of us know that no society can effectively legislate and enforce the morality of one's conscience and moral codes of conduct. Morality must be taught and exemplified in family structures and reinforced in religious and educational institutions. For this reason alone, systemic racism has become a "behind closed doors" structural activity rather than blatant and overt institutionalized exclusion. Negative racist constructs have always been instituted by a few ungodly men and given to the masses in order to make its tenets effective. Behind-the-scenes racism exists primarily because of the ungodly nature of the white male power structure.

Recent violent events in American society reveal that there is a need for morally based, godly spirituality in our culture and institutional social structure. American society is coming unglued. The need for social cohesion in American society is obvious even to casual observers. For example, armed men should not murder unarmed individuals due to race-based assumptions. Children should not be killed in public schools, movie theaters, and other public venues. Constructing legal scenarios (e.g., Stand Your Ground laws) in order to justify murder in the name of law and order is unacceptable. Women should not be raped on college campuses. Legalizing sin, calling it a democratic tenet of equality, is equally unacceptable.

The Christian church is the only hope for the salvation of American society because America was established as one nation under God with liberty and justice for all. American politics has become confusion on top of more confusion because of political polarization. The task that confronts American culture is simply this: how do we learn to live from a godly understanding of the Bible, rather than individualized understanding? Power is a shared resource.

Here's where the Christian church can play a profound role in helping to develop a focused, godly moral imperative: by keeping with God's will of loving Him and loving each other, because God's will is only realized through love and service to others. And herein is the moral failure of "white" institutional Christianity. The Christian church has failed universally because the church is being used for personal agendas, rather than God's agenda of Heaven on earth, not hell on earth. Evil exists because good individuals are truly the silent majority. When pastoral leaders do not preach conscience-based sermons, they invariably allow parishioners to become immoral pew-warmers.

Some pastors are afraid to preach morally based sermons that creatively address the issues of systemic racism and classism for fear of losing their pastoral positions of power based upon money. All "isms" are schisms and schisms divide. America is truly the most segregated nation on the planet every Sunday at eleven o'clock. The question remains: why does this exist?

Some black Christian churches have failed to effectively address the spiritual issues of social acceptability and moral respectability. Therefore, simply preaching sermons based upon emotionalism for monetary gain enslaves churches (pastors and parishioners) to vulgar materialism and political non-sense. Politics is in the church, but politics should not be of the church. Politics should maximize the common good in our culture by honoring the godly tenets of the Bible. On the one hand, black pastors take parishioners to the Cross and they leave them there. That is, black pastors get Jesus up, but they do not get the flock up; they don't empower individuals to become self-sufficient, self-reliant, and spiritually/materially productive in their communities.

On the other hand, white pastors are good at teaching and exemplifying self-discipline, self-sufficiency, and self-responsibility, but rarely, if ever, go to the Cross, much less take their parishioners there. At the Cross, there is universal sin, common humanity, graveyard destiny, collective responsibility, and human interdependence, that is, the notion that I am my brother's keeper.

Everything of this world must be done decently and in order (1 Corinthians 14:40). There is a season for all things, but God's Word never changes (Matthew 24:35). Pastoral leaders in America must understand: "Be not deceived: evil communications corrupt good manners. Awake to righteousness, and sin not; for some have not the knowledge of God: I speak this to your shame" (1 Corinthians: 15:33-34). American pastoral leaders are called to: "Sanctify them through thy truth: thy word is truth" (John 17:17). I beseech you, pastoral leaders, in the name of Jesus, teach and preach the Bible and we will have peace on earth and good will toward all men. For, if we do the will of God, God will make a way to peace out of no way. God, our heavenly Father, we pray for peace in America and peace between all nations. Peace without moral order is no peace at all. So be it!

3 | *American Family Life*

Numerous recent national events have revealed alarming and disturbing indications about where American society is headed culturally. Society begins and ends within the family unit. God instituted the family unit as the basis for human social existence and spiritual salvation. When God gave Noah the "rainbow sign," He saved four families, not eight individuals. Abraham Lincoln said it rightly: "A nation divided against itself cannot stand." Therefore, the root cause of division in American culture is twofold: the breakdown of the family unit and institutional Christianity's inability to develop a focused social and moral imperative about the meaning of life.

Of course, external economic constraints have radically altered family life in America. For example, our movement from an industrial economy to a service economy to an information technology economy has radically altered the character of family structure as well as family life. Unfortunately, family life is mirroring the values of the corporate business structure rather than divine intent. When family life is defined solely in economic terms, quality of life is universally affected. The first order of business for public policy decision makers should be to usher in a redefinition of the family as a spiritual unit rather than an economic unit.

There is an old, time-honored adage that goes like this: "The family that prays together stays together." Praying together is about family self-introspection, that is, the teaching and exemplifying of spiritual precepts and concepts from the Bible. An individual comes to an understanding of the true meaning of life within the family unit. Of course, the environment surrounding the family plays an important role in the process as well. It takes far more than a village to help raise a child; it takes state and federal governments as well, because the understanding of a village just might be too narrow.

The task that confronts American culture is simply this: How do we learn to live together with a godly understanding of the Bible, rather than individual self-centeredness? A civilized society knows how to agree to disagree without conducting its disagreements through the barrel of guns, guns, and more guns. In other words, a civilized society knows how to make moral decisions about how we should live.

Of course, learning how to resolve conflict non-violently begins within family units. For example, because all individuals have the power of their unique personalities, individual free-will power is not a zero-sum game. Power is a shared resource. Here's where Christianity can play a major role in developing a focused moral imperative by teaching and exemplifying the two greatest commandments ever written: loving God and loving each other.

The confusion within the family context is charged to our children because they will suffer the consequences of this confusion. For, after all, to save our children, parents, public policy professionals, teachers and public school administrators must issue this challenge to the nation's children:

- As a student, I choose to love myself, and therefore become my best friend so that I might learn to love and respect others.
- I choose to develop my mind, because my mind is my only defense against exploitation by myself or others, and more importantly, my mind is the key to self-discipline and self-moderation.
- I choose to have positive life goals, because life is about choices and choices have consequences, whether good or bad.

Without a doubt, the church is God's house of prayer, and it is in churches that the spiritual meaning of family life ought to be illuminated and strengthened. Therefore, the church has an important healing role to play in this process. Of course, finding creative ways to make family life religious is a collective societal responsibility, and local churches ought to view it as their responsibility to help strengthen families one by one.

4 | *The Prophet Hosea's Story*

The marriage of Hosea to a prostitute is about God's love for us, not the Prophet Hosea. Think about this question: Is America treating God just like a whore? God loves America, God has blessed America, and of course, Americans should not be treating God like a whore. A physical church building on every corner is not a solution to immorality. Building church monuments to ourselves and not to the glory of God is an absolute abomination to God. Self-centered millionaires and billionaires tearing down and building bigger barns for their own selfish-aggrandizement when in the twinkling of an eye their souls might be required of them is shameful. Hosea's wife was bold in her whorish exploits and would leave home and come back and brag about her exploits with other men.

Gomer even had children by other men. Yet, Hosea loved Gomer and tried in vain to reason with her in her wrongdoing. He would even allow her to return home and would forgive her transgressions. God loves and forgives America and He expects us to do things decently and in order. "Be not deceived; God is not mocked: for whatsoever a man soweth, that shall he also reap" (Galatians 4:7). This is called the "law of reciprocity" because what goes up must come down. And, of course, what goes around comes around.

In the final analysis, God changed Gomer and she became a good and faithful wife. God's love for us is just like that of Hosea for his prostitute wife, Gomer. "For God so loved the world, that He gave his only begotten Son, that whosoever believeth in him should not perish, but have everlasting life" (John 3:16). The story of the Prophet Hosea is a profound and compassionate love story. "The beginning of the word of the Lord to Hosea. And the Lord said to Hosea, Go, take unto thee a wife of whoredoms and children of whoredoms: for the land hath committed great whoredom, departing from the Lord." I propose another question for you to think about: Have blacks and America committed whoredom by departing from the Word of God? At one time, blacks were the most faithful Christians in America, because Christianity and theology were the spiritual bridge that brought blacks over the troubled waters of institutional racism. Blacks were given a religion that they did not understand to make them "happy slaves." Work hard for "master," be a good slave, and you will receive your reward in Heaven, not on earth. However, God freed blacks through the same religion their slave masters practiced and you know the rest of the story. Without a doubt, Christianity (that is, the Black church) was all in all for the Black community. Shame, shame, and more shame on those doubled-minded individuals who recognize the church is still the center of the Black community, but put *self-interest* first, while the needs of the Black community go lacking. All Christians know, that God sees us before we see ourselves and God will not stand for the church of Jesus Christ being prostituted.

If the Book of Hosea in the Holy Bible sounds like what is taking place in the Black community and American society in general, then you are correct in your thinking. If you thought that we had trouble with dope, just wait until we universally legalize sin as a civil rights issue. Pandora's Box will be wide open. If this resonates true in the heart of your mind, blink your eyes and say, 'Amen, Amen, and Amen!' That is, say, 'Amen' for the Holy Trinity. Without a doubt, we cannot overcome what is going on in America by continuously engaging in sin.

There is no hope in dope and no salvation in "legalizing" sin. Nancy Reagan declared that America should "just say no to dope." Today, America should just say "no" to legalized sin. Selfishness and the love of money are destroying the social fabric of American society. Bad decision making and passing bad laws are taking America over the moral bankruptcy cliff. "Lay hands suddenly on no man, neither be partaker of other men's sin: keep thyself pure" (1 Timothy 5:22). God-fearing individuals are in the world, but are called not to be of the world. "Be not deceived: evil communications corrupt good manners" (1 Corinthians 15:33). Talking about legalizing sin is definitely evil communication.

America must repent of her sins against God and if America does not repent it's over; even though God always saves his own. During the Great Flood, God saved four families which included Noah and his children. Sticking with God is a sure shot! Otherwise, your sins will definitely be revealed. Sin is lawlessness because *all* sin is unrighteousness.

The Christian church is the only salvation for America because God respects morality. However, there is only one church and that is the church of our living Savior Jesus Christ (the Holy Trinity). In twenty-first century America, every Joe Moe Blow has his church, and not the church of the living Savior. Building church houses on every street corner is not the basis for a sound economic system. This state of affairs is helping America continue to function in a state of confusion and disorder. First Corinthians 14:33 states, "For God is not the author of confusion, but of peace, as in all churches of the saints."

The prophet Hosea personally experienced how God feels when he loves us and desires the best for us through a relationship with Jesus Christ, but we allow the devil to play tricks with our minds about the things of this world. There is a lot of whoredom going on in America. Let's stop prostituting God for our own selfish, vain needs.

Where do we go from here? I hope not to hell in a hand-basket. "For we are saved by hope: for what a man seeth, why doth he yet hope for? But if we hope for that we see not, then do we with patience wait for it" (Romans 8: 24-25). Too many blacks are not looking back and reaching back the way we did when the physical signs of demarcation-limitation were vividly posted. The physical signs have been taken down for some time now and too many blacks are comfortable in their self-serving materialistic exploits and the Black community suffers. Therefore, the sense of a tight knit Black community is a thing of the past. Wickedness will not stand because any sin against the body is an abomination to God and godly principles. For example, eating too much of the wrong types of foods is a sin, since the Bible contains dietary laws. Get right, Black community! Things are severely out of order. Let's fix them before it's too late. Selah.

5 | *Why Blacks and Whites Do Not Worship Together*

There is only one God and He is the only one who has the right to play God because He is God. "God is Spirit and they that worship Him must worship Him in Spirit and Truth." Whites are not God. Blacks are not God. Skin color is not the deciding factor for salvation because God is no respecter of persons or color. God is God all by Himself because He is the source of all things. Without a doubt, physical death is the social equalizer in the equation between whites and blacks as well as males and females. Spiritual death is altogether another issue.

Why don't blacks and whites worship together? In

my opinion, there are two overriding primary reasons: (A) White institutionalization of the notion of white superiority, and (B) different worship styles based on distinctive cultural traditions. When we cannot tell the truth to ourselves, we obviously cannot tell the truth to others. Here lies the crux of the spiritual problem: the segregated Body of Christ is not being absolutely honest with one another. Whites lie to other whites. Blacks lie to other blacks. As a result, individuals seeking to control the "truth" often cause us to end-up in a state of confusion.

White pastors generally *teach* self-reliance and self-discipline through God. Black pastors emotionally *preach* that God will do everything and no self-discipline or self-motivation is required. Free-will makes God not a divine Santa Claus. Prayer without works is dead. White pastors in general take the guilty stain off parishioners and Black pastors place the guilty stain on parishioners. That is, Black pastors preach what they understand to be the most important thing about living and the spiritual rite of passage: salvation and being born-again.

Experiential life styles and family differences are evident in the content of sermons, and delivery styles in black and white churches are vastly different. These facts also account for different motives for worship and church attendance. Without a doubt, both White and Black pastors are very loose and free with their interpretation of the Word of God.

Church attendance in the White community is about perpetuating cultural Whiteness (societal and family traditions). Church attendance in the Black community is about perpetuating cultural Blackness based on the dehumanization of Blackness. God and godly living are left out of the worship equation. Worshiping God ought to be about individuals understanding godly principles and spirituality, not racial and cultural glorification. Praising God is for glorification of the goodness of God. God is good all the time and He is greatly to be praised. To be sure, "God judgeth the righteous, and God is angry with the wicked every day" (Psalm 7:11).

Church attendance in both the Black and White communities should be influenced by Christ's earthly example of love and service. These are real methods of worship for a living God who redeems humanity, cares for humanity, and, above all, forgives us of our sins. When this takes place, both blacks and whites can praise God from whom all blessings flow together in love, peace, and joy. Then and only then, will worship become our faithful service and an expression of godly love for each other.

"Shopping is physical and worship is spiritual." "In Black churches it's all about naming and claiming it, the gospel of prosperity. In White churches it's about tearing down cathedrals (barns) and building bigger cathedrals to stand tall and proud without bowing down to anyone, including God." But, we know in the twinkling of an eye an individual's soul could be required. Both declarations are based on false premises.

Values and social barriers that are deep-rooted in cultural differences and family traditions are difficult to break down and, of course, some of them are good, but they are not of God. A lot of what goes on in both Black and Whites churches has absolutely nothing to do with God. In fact, in many twenty-first century churches there is no reverence for God. This is why Blacks and Whites can party together on Saturday night, but cannot worship God together on Sunday morning. Clearly, we are not serving the same God. Even on Sundays, we shop in shopping malls together. Why can't we worship God together in Christian churches?

On the one hand, whites have been free all of their lives and indeed American society was established for whites to experience individual and family-related success. While, on the other hand, America was designed for blacks to serve whites. Unfortunately, some whites still feel the American social system gives them superiority over blacks. A case in point: the vulgar disrespect displayed by some Whites toward the Office of the President simply because a Black man is the president. Whatever happened to the principle of respect for the position even if you have contempt for the individual who holds the position?

In twenty-first century America, far too many Americans do not want to follow the principles of God for spiritual salvation. Often we are not worshiping God in the Spirit, but men in the flesh. In some situations church attendance has simply become a best-dressed contest, not an occasion for holiness. There is nothing wrong with giving God your best, even in dress; but when its importance supersedes that of worshiping a holy and just God, then it becomes a vain idol.

Sin is a spiritual problem. Institutional racism is a spiritual problem that creates a sin-hatred chasm. Racism has oriented life in American society toward skin color rather than toward God, godly living, and spiritual understanding; therefore, hatred is the primary reason Blacks and whites cannot worship together. As a result, the objective on both sides of the aisle is to perpetuate racial and cultural distinctiveness, rather than God-centered Christianity and godly living. But, we all know, that all of us are God's children.

God hates racism. Hatred creates separation from God and, above all, it creates societal confusion. There is no hatred in Heaven and, therefore, no need for a Civil Rights Movement. Having peace in all the churches of the saints will invariably stop our insatiable desire to prostitute the church of Jesus Christ for personal reasons; glorifying God, the Creator of all things, excluding skin-color, will be our united mission. So be it.

Reading Is Developmental

6

Reading is developmental, not just fundamental. Reading is about comprehension, analytical thinking, and spiritual/intellectual understanding. Reading forces an individual to think about *thinking*. The time-proven fundamental basis for the acquisition of knowledge and understanding is reading (self-improvement). "Blessed is he that readeth, and they that hear the words of this prophecy, and keep those things which are written therein: for the time is at hand" (Revelation 1:3). Why is it that most Americans, especially minority Americans, are not reading?

Modern technology has produced a double-edged sword cultural narrative primarily because television has had the negative impact of pulling individuals, especially children, away from books. Most Americans are no longer reading the Bible, books, newspapers, or other printed materials. The founding fathers created a mass universal education system that Americans might primarily be able to read the Bible. College and university students do not read books because they are too busy texting and eye-balling their cell phones. As a result, four-year college graduation rates have declined. Most importantly, college students know very little about the text in the "Book of Life" from Genesis to Revelation. (Bible is an acronym for: Basic Instructions Before Leaving Earth). The golden age of television is becoming not so golden after all. Technology, especially television, has fueled the dumbing-down of American culture (instant gratification). Consequently, long form thinking is becoming a skill of the past. For society to solve complicated social problems and find medical cures for deadly diseases, long range thinking and planning are an intellectual necessity. Thus, reading is the primary intellectual foundation for creative/critical thinking.

Individuals are not reading, for the most part, because

they have not been taught how to read phonetically (phonics). Developmental reading begins in the family structure, which should provide the basic priority experience; children do not read books, because they do not see their parents reading books. Yet, not being able to read is not a crime, but at the same time not desiring to know how to read is a sin, not only against one's self but against one's children. If parents cannot read and know whether or not the elocution of Scriptures are being rightly divided, then they may be easily misled. "For I rejoiced greatly, when the brethren came and testified of the truth that is in thee, even as thou walkest in the truth" (1 John 1:3). Simply put, man's interpretation of this Scripture is: "If you talk the talk, you must walk the walk." There is nothing new under the sun, but an individual must know how to read so he or she can understand this spiritual and moral lesson. Ignorance of the law is no excuse. This spiritual law of "reaping what you sow" comes directly from the Bible: "For the invisible things of him from the creation of the world are clearly seen, being understood by the things that are made, even his eternal power and God-head; so that they are without excuse…" (Romans 1: 20-21).

Knowing how to simply read in a democratic society is essential to being a productive citizen, because democracy is for an intelligent citizenry. Reading is about creative thinking. It has rightly been said that a picture is worth a thousand words. On the other hand, a good book is worth a thousand ideas. Ideas make the world go around, and not money. Ideas not only make money, but also become life-saving ventures. Holiness makes the spiritual world go around, and makes for peace on earth and good will towards all.

Reading the Bible is an important spiritual-intellectual life experience, because the categories of understanding are spiritual and moral in nature: time, class, number, and space. Reading requires creative thinking about the spiritual meaning of life (self-discipline). The Bible is the book of life the basis for spiritual self-development, because there is nothing new under the sun. "The thing that hath been, it is that which shall be; and that which is done is that which shall be done: and there is no new thing under the sun" (Ecclesiastes 1:9). Herein lies the creative roles of both theology and sociology as academic disciplines. By the way, President Abraham Lincoln constantly read the Bible, and this just might be the major reason for the Emancipation Proclamation.

It seems as though American society is becoming an

anti-intellectual culture; that is, America has become an entertainment-oriented culture (external-subliminal stimulation). Conditioning our children toward visual stimulation (entertainment) and away from books is a recipe for spiritual-moral decadence. Entertainment is not self-development. Reading is spiritual self-development. Should we be worried? Yes, because our children are not being prepared academically for the challenges of higher education. As a result, embracing the STEM (Science, Technology, Engineering, and Math) disciplines has become a no-no. Far too many of our children are not disciplined in abstract thinking, because abstract thinking is an essential requirement in "STEM" fields of study. Allowing our children to be entertained by technology (screen-age-baby-sitting-services), especially the television, is an unwise and extremely harmful parenting proposition.

Reading the Bible with clarity helps individuals understand all of life's spiritual challenges. If it is not in the Bible, it does not exist. The question of questions is: Can we save ourselves from ourselves by reading more? The answer is a resounding yes; yes, we can, in this writer's opinion. During slavery, reading was a precious spiritual-intellectual commodity, because a high price-tag was placed upon it – one's life. Now, individuals can freely read, but they don't. Simply put, too many Blacks have become captives of their own intellectual inability to understand and take ownership for their own socio-economic condition. Some whites created a "Black dehumanization system" where all whites are beneficiaries and all blacks with God's help must resolve the problem.

This writer confesses that we need to strengthen our families, our churches, and our educational institutions, because even with less we have achieved and can achieve even more by learning how to read, learning how to work together, and above all learning how to love and serve each other. Selah!

Education Is
7 | Still the Key

The parameters of educational development in the twenty-first century are not what they were in the nineteenth century. The classic argument of Booker T. Washington and W.E.B. Dubois is still relevant in the age of information technology. The "talented tenth versus trade skill development" was an either/or argument during their era. The twenty-first century argument demands an approach that includes both educational concepts.

A quality education for all children is the civil rights issue of the twenty-first century, especially for minority children. Public schooling must be based upon the philosophy of children first, and if children are first, then no child is left behind. "No child left behind" is only half of the equation. "No parent left behind" completes the equation. In some instances, public schools must begin to provide educational parenting skill classes in the evenings, especially for single-parent families.

It is extremely difficult for teachers to teach undisciplined children. It is unfortunate that undisciplined children do not understand the importance of social conduct and civil behavior in the school environment as it relates to learning. Churches must shoulder more of the spiritual responsibility for assisting single parents with moral educational issues. Too many Black children are growing up without the ability to internally discipline themselves. And, of course, when law enforcement officials discipline, it is usually with physical force and sometimes deadly force. The moral relationship between the educational process, getting along with fellow classmates, and, above all, respecting teachers, is an essential part of learning. Of course, internal moral discipline should first be taught in homes.

A quality education in American society is a necessity, not a luxury. Reading is an essential disciplinary tool in moral integration, in intellectual integration, and, above all, in social integration. Integrating ideas about the meaning of life is essential to social and political integration. If an individual is on the battlefield for the LORD, political correctness should not be the battle-cry. It is a sad state of affairs in American society that reading is not a priority, especially among Black youth. Opening a book from time to time is a moral imperative.

We live in a global economy that is based upon information technology because the computer has become an academic learning center. Upon completing high school, American students will be competing with students from around the world (e.g., England, France, Japan, China, and even students from the continent of Africa). The world does not accept or respect excuses. Black students must learn to celebrate the dream of what it means to be created in the "image of God," and above all, realize that they can do all things through God when faith in God is the substance of things hoped for. "Yes, I can. Yes, I will."

The objective is to have a significant life, not just experience success in life. To have a significant life an individual must have these eternal-internal values and character traits:

- Self-love. Happiness and joy must be experienced within a family context. Family is the first school, first church, and the beginning of society.
- Peace of mind. You cannot buy peace of mind or happiness in department stores. Shopping is not a recipe for happiness or a successful life; it is only a recipe for spending money that you do not have.
- Temperance (self-discipline and self-control). Individuals must learn to temper themselves or else vanity will destroy them. An individual cannot have everything he wants when he wants it. Life is not that simplistic. Moral education and intellectual education are flip-sides of the same coin.

Jesus told us to always anticipate the consequences of one's own actions because there is a price tag on everything we say and do. An individual cannot get something in life for nothing. If you want something for nothing, then you want nothing, and nothing from nothing invariably leaves nothing. All individuals who dance to the music must pay the piper. Individuals can pay as they enter. Or individuals can pay as they leave. But, pay you must. Ask yourself the following question: How do I live with myself as well as in relationship with others? An important follow-up question would be: What am I willing to sacrifice to live the way I say I want to live?

Americans must find reasonable solutions to our educational dilemma. A beginning point just might be integrating ideas about the meaning of life. Too many teachers are simply "showing-up and picking-up" checks when work should come before money and pleasure.

Democracy requires an intelligent citizenry because democracy cannot exist with an ignorant citizenry, therefore, reading is essential and fundamental.

We must first teach our children to pray for wisdom. Wisdom is associated with good understanding. Knowledge, therefore, is derived from a good understanding. King Solomon said it best: "Rather a good understanding than silver or gold" (Proverbs 16:16). "Make your ear attentive to wisdom; incline your heart to understanding" (Proverbs 2:2). Without a doubt, individuals perish because of a lack of vision. Inquiring minds desire to know the truth, because it is truth that will make you free.

On the other hand, there are many among us who have degrees and keys down to their knees, but have no spiritual-sense. Spiritual common sense is not common. We have become a nation of change, but the change is not always associated with civilized moral behavior. Selah!

Attitude is About Beatitudes

8

Attitude is the spiritual foundation of human interaction and social life, and a major influence on both moral character and civil behavior. It is difficult to change attitudes, because environmental circumstances must be spiritually altered as well. This is why attitude is about the spiritual Beatitudes recorded in Holy Scriptures; Jesus taught the twelve disciples these basic principles of virtue and morality. American society is on the moral decline because the spiritual qualities of the Beatitudes are lacking in individual consciousness. Too many Americans have a lack of spiritual understanding concerning family as the basic unit of society, the spiritual role of

Christian churches, the role of educational institutions in undergirding democratic-moral tenets, and the decline of spirituality and civility in political governance.

Jesus clearly understood the importance of spiritual attitude, and this is precisely why He taught the disciples the Beatitudes, which mean: "Be of this attitude" (Luke 6:20-38). Bad attitudes produce bad behaviors, and bad behaviors produce bad consequences.

- "Blessed be ye poor: for yours is the Kingdom of God." When individuals do the will of God, Heaven and earth are the same (The Lord's Prayer). Many are poor physically, but rich spiritually, because the righteous do not have to beg for bread.
- "Blessed are ye that hunger now: for ye shall be filled. Blessed are ye that weep now: for ye shall laugh." If individuals hunger for God's Word (Truth), they shall be filled with the Holy Spirit.
- "Blessed are ye when men hate you, and they shall separate you from their company, and shall reproach you, and cast out your name as evil, for the Son of Man's sake." The world cannot

handle the Truth.

- "But woe unto to you that are rich! For you have received your consultation." A rich man can go to Heaven, but it's difficult for a rich man to go to Heaven just as it is difficult for a camel to go through the eye of a needle (Matthew 19:24).

- "Woe unto you who are full! For ye shall hunger. Woe to you who laugh now! For ye shall mourn and weep." Life consists of swift transitions; therefore, individuals must learn how to spiritually adapt to both good as well as bad circumstances.

- "Woe unto you, when all men shall speak well of you! So did their fathers to the false prophets. But I say unto you which hear, love your enemies, do good to them which hate you, bless them that curse you, and pray for them that despitefully use you. And unto him that smiteth thee on one cheek offer also the other; and him that taketh away thy cloak forbid not to take thy coat also." Individual attitudes and social behaviors must be balanced spiritually.

- "Whoever hits you on one cheek, offer him the other also; and whoever takes away your coat, do not withhold your shirt from him either." Individuals must always be willing to go the extra mile spiritually.

- "Give to every man that asketh of thee; and of him that taketh away thy goods ask them not again. And as ye would that men should do to you, do ye also to them likewise." If you want a friend, you must know how to be a spiritual friend. Jesus modeled this in His relationships throughout the New Testament. What a friend we have in Jesus!

- "For if ye love them which love you, what thanks have ye? For sinners also love those that love them." Unconditional love is what God requires.

- "And if ye lend to them of whom ye hope to receive, what thanks have ye? For sinners also lend to sinners, to receive as much again." Give with spiritual understanding expecting our reward to be with our Lord.

- "But I say unto you which hear, Love your enemies, do good to them which hate you, bless them that curse you, and pray for them which despitefully use you." In doing so, an individual heaps hot coals upon them.

- "Be ye therefore merciful, as your Father also is merciful." Spiritual generosity is a Christian expectation.

- "Judge not, and ye shall not be judged: condemn not, and you shall not be condemned: forgive, and you shall be forgiven." God judges, and as Christians, we should inspect our lives utilizing these two spiritual witnesses. Never let the sun go down on your unforgiveness (anger).

- "Give and it shall be given unto you; good measure, pressed down, shaken together, and running over, shall men give into your bosom. For with the same measure that you mete withal it shall be measured to you again." There is no secret what God can do: "Be not deceived: God is not mocked: for whatsoever a man soweth, that shall he also reap" (Galatians: 6:7).

The Beatitudes are about spiritual values (virtue) and social behavior. If our youth were taught the beatitudes, American society would be better served. In the age to come (last days), there will be a reversal of values, because individuals will have waxed cold, seeking to make right wrong and wrong right, and make it work for their own personal-social dysfunctions. "And it is appointed unto men once to die, but after this the judgment" (Hebrew 9:27). Simply put, "God judgeth the righteous, and God is angry with the wicked every day" (Psalm 7:11).

God gave us the "Beatitudes" as spiritual directives for how we ought to live in peace and harmony, that is in fellowship with each other, and try to understand each other's pain and suffering. Without a doubt, "There is a way which seemeth right unto a man; but the end thereof are the ways of death" (Proverbs 14: 12). Self-centeredness has become a monumental problem in America. Selah!

9 How to Win With a Bad Hand

Black Americans have been dealt a bad hand because of their skin color simply because whites have arbitrarily made life about skin color. But, of course, blacks spiritually know that life is about moral character and intellectual integrity, not about skin color. Therefore, blacks in general do not view their skin color as having been dealt a bad hand. Of course, this is why many blacks live meaningful lives despite institutional restrictions because of their skin color.

The human mind is God's most precious gift to individuals. Indeed, the mind is delicate and even frail. Human will is also a precious gift from God. Lack of motivation, inadequate discipline, and the absence of personal integrity can do to one's mind what lack of exercise and improper eating habits can do to one's physical health. Having a worldly mind rather than a spiritual mind in a racially-oriented society just might leave you with a bad hand. Making life a continuing learning experience is largely a matter of developing the mind. Therefore, if an individual is not developing a spiritually positive mindset, he may well be creating a formidable foe: himself. After all, an individual's mind is his best defense against dehumanization and exploitation. Character is about spiritual and internal values rather than material and external values. Life is about the choices we make. This is precisely why you can win even when you are dealt a bad hand "societally" because of skin color. Life is choice-driven. Choices have consequences: good and bad. Without a doubt, America has dealt blacks a bad hand called institutional racism.

Here's the formula for how to win with a bad hand:

- Face your fears. If at first you do not succeed, try, try, and try again.
- Forget your failures. Press on toward the high calling modeled in the life of Jesus Christ.
- Take ownership of your own destiny. It is not about what happens to you, but how you

respond to what happens to you. Individuals cannot always control what happens, but we can control how we respond to what happens.

- It is not cool to be stupid or dumb. Success comes by making the right life choices. Success does not come to you; you must go after it.
- Where there is predictability, there is also stability and accountability.

It's self-assessment time in the Black community: it's housecleaning time in the Black community. The personal baggage of some of our political and pastoral leaders is getting in the way of a healthy Black community institutionally. It's church cleaning time. The institutional church is too important to the well-being of the Black community to be dysfunctional. Institutional Christianity should be about spiritual and moral character development, not money-making schemes.

How do we repair the lives of churchgoers so that they might live spiritually creative and productive lives? That is, how do we share the love of God that was expressed in how Jesus lived and in the way He died? In other words, how can we have the Heaven on earth that was articulated in the Lord's Prayer?

It is also political leadership accountability time in the Black community. Our political leaders sometimes forget that they were elected by the people to give the people a voice in political matters. God anoints them and allows them to become leaders in our community. They should not take their responsibilities lightly because they are accountable, not only to the people, but also to God.

God is God and there is none other beside Him. His sovereignty is unquestionable. He is God and there is nothing impossible with God. With God there is no such thing as a bad hand. The question is: Who is on the Lord's side? In the twenty-first century, far too many individuals in the Black community seem to be operating on the devil's side.

A perpetual question that searches the heart of man is: "Who do you want, Jesus or Barabbas?" Think before answering, because Barabbas was a patriot and Jesus was the Savior! There are many patriots, but only one Savior. Black on Black crime has become a vulgar and shameful expression of cannibalism (i.e., internalized self-hatred). Of course, this state of affairs exists because of a lack of self-discipline and institutional moral integrity. May God help the Black church to return to a righteous posture for the benefit of our communities, becoming a bright light in a dark world that shines beyond geographical boundaries into the hearts of all men.

The classic example of how to win with a bad hand is the Biblical saga between David and King Saul (1 Samuel chapters 1-22). Blacks can win even with a bad hand, because whatever the skin color, the key to a successful life, rather than success in life, is learning how to make you, your best friend.

Black history begins with a positive "Who am I?" experience within the family context. If your individual answer to this state of affairs is, "I am a child of God," then you can make your own history, not becoming a pleasure-seeker, hero-worshipper, and above all, one who seeks to keep up with the "Joneses." All history is salvation history; that is, God seeking to give every individual eternal life. Black history should never become hero-worship. Learning to make you, your best friend is the key to a successful life. Success is not in material possessions, because life is not found in the abundance of things. Individuals are born naked and leave only with the skin they came wrapped in, because their relatives will not allow them to leave with material goodies.

Blacks are the most influential socio-economic group in American society and, therefore, are an integral part of American society. For Blacks today to alleviate their victimization status because of their economic position in American society, they must make spiritual changes in their homes, churches, educational institutions, and politics. Without a doubt, Blacks need to come together with a clear spiritual understanding, "That all things must be done decently and in order"—God's order. We need spiritual unity and a renaissance in all of our basic institutions. And, at the same time, America needs divine intervention to restore her to her godly purpose. Only then will Blacks truly see the "salvation" of the Lord manifested in this nation.

Relationships versus Situations

10

Relationships are spiritual in nature, whereas situations are based on instant gratification, entertainment, pleasure seeking moments, and vanity. Relationships precede situations in time and space, because they are about spiritual commitments and obligations, that is, spiritually expectation driven and long term in nature. Interpersonal interactions are about the spiritual values and commitments that are recorded in Galatians 5:22-24: "But the fruit of the Spirit is love, joy, peace, longsuffering, gentleness, goodness, faith, meekness, temperance: against such there is no law." Another Scripture cited below also addresses the spiritual basis for all "forms and types" of interrelationships: "If we walk in the light, as he is in the *light*, we have fellowship one with another, and the blood of Jesus Christ his son cleanseth us from all sin" (1 John 1:17). Of course, we must understand that, through faith, Jesus Christ is the spiritual mediator for our sins before the throne of God (1 Timothy 2:5). Interpersonal interactions are about spiritual fellowship with each other. The word "light" in this Biblical scriptural context implies truth.

Ultimately, life is about spiritual relationships and commitments. What are you committed to? Is it selfishness, greed, envy, personality conflicts, or jealousy? Life is about "spiritual-sameness" in God, not seeking pleasure-sameness in the world. Relationships have spiritual commitments associated with them. However, God does not want individuals to become so heavenly bound that they are no earthly good.

Situational experiences and situation-ethics have torn down the moral walls of American society, because there is no commitment involved in these kinds of experiences. In the twenty-first century, any and everything goes for the sake of maximizing the pleasure principle. It is spiritually recorded, "But she that liveth in pleasure is dead while she liveth" (1

Timothy 5:6). Life is not about pleasure; but redemptive suffering, that is, suffering for the sake of the truth. Pleasure seeking is the beginning of unnatural lusts. Individuals should never allow lusts of the flesh to control their thought processes. "What! Know ye not that your body is the temple of the Holy Ghost which is in you, which ye have of God, and ye are not your own? For ye are bought with a price: therefore glorify God in your body, and in your spirit, which are God's" (1 Corinthians 6:19-20).

Situations are usually about maximizing the pleasure principle, especially sexual pleasure. This state of affairs has produced untold societal confusion: fornication, unwanted pregnancies, adultery, workplace sexual confusion, sexually transmitted diseases, and personal hardship situations. Human sexuality is a gift from God simply because sexuality is spiritual in nature and involves personal choices. However, because of the pleasure-seeking principle, we have turned the "gift of God" into a sinful physical pleasure-seeking activity sometimes referred to using the F-word.

All of this spiritual confusion has created a situation-ethics oriented-society. And, of course, this spiritual confusion is charged to our children as well as future generations. When individuals devalue each other as spiritual beings, instant gratification moments (secular humanism) become the basis for interpersonal interactions, whereas, relationships have eternal spiritual expectations and commitments associated with them.

Situations only produce zombies, and no individual wants to become an imitator. Relationships produce spiritual individuals like Moses, King David, King Solomon, Dr. Martin L. King, Jr., Harriet Tubman, Mary M. Bethune, and First Lady Michelle Obama.

American society has become spiritually sick, especially in the Black community. When individuals abandon the spiritual covering of God, the moral walls are pulled down, and of course, God pulls the curtain down on the final act. In my opinion, the only hope for restoration of American culture is in the Christian church and through self-educational development. The church, especially in the Black community, must get right with God. It must cut-out the emotional-oriented foolishness and spiritualize church-goers rather than entertain them. Again, the Christian church in the Black community must get right with God and fly right.

Black churches must institutionalize "positive-modeling-behaviors" for young Black men on how to be a man, simply because God has spiritually commanded that a man must "work by the sweat of your brow" (Genesis 3:17-19). Above all, Black churches must help young females learn how to become godly ladies, because the world will teach them how to become the W-word or the B-word. "But she that liveth in pleasure is dead while she liveth" (1 Timothy 5:6). This is an extremely important church-related spiritual endeavor because of the alarming statistics associated with the breakdown of the family and out-of-wedlock births. More importantly, women are the carriers of culture. Hence forth, God has said to women because of disobedience, "I will greatly multiply thy sorrow and thy conception; in sorrow thou shalt bring forth children; and thy desire shall be to thy husband, and he shall rule over thee" (Genesis 3:16).

"Be not deceived; God is not mocked: for whatsoever a man soweth, that shall he also reap. For he that soweth to his flesh shall of his flesh reap corruption; but he that soweth to the Spirit shall of the Spirit reap life everlasting. And let us not be weary in well doing: for in due season we shall reap, if we faint not" (Galatians 6: 7-9). "Sometimes a situation can get an individual in a situation." Selah!

What's Going On?

11

In the twentieth century, a famous (flawed human being) singer, Marvin Gaye, asked the question, "What's going on?" This question is still relevant today, in twenty-first century America, because we are moving from one confused moral state of existence to a higher level of moral confusion; there seems to be no end in sight. This is why we must become spiritually intelligent enough to understand the solution (answer) to the question, because whatever is "going on" is not good for American society.

Subsequently, we are more segregated and politically divided today than we were prior to the passage of the 1964 Civil Rights Act and the 1965 Voting Rights Act (Jim Crow Era). The question is, why? What's going on in America? In part, the answers lie in these socio-economic-political-religious realities:

- The breakdown of the nuclear family structure. Too many children being born out of wedlock is a serious spiritual, moral, and societal problem that must be remedied. Children must be taught character development traits and spiritual values at home, before going to church and school. Tough love must be exemplified in the home environment. Children must be given positive modeling behavior responsibilities in their home environments.
- Educational institutions are allowing too much of the societal instant-gratification confusion to influence the structure of schooling, which in turn, influences educational development (thought processes). This has produced the me, myself, and I syndrome. The human mind is our greatest resource, and not enough economic capital goes into the development of minds and hearts (attitudes). We need a better quality of professional teaching in our educational institutions, and teachers who have the spiritual desire and professional ability to motivate, develop, and inspire the students entrusted to their care.

- The current two-party political system has divided America by race/ethnicity, social class, religion, and gender, even so much so that some seek to keep "certain" individuals from exercising their Constitutional sacred right to vote. Lest we forget, charity begins at home, and then spreads abroad. This in and of itself creates political governing confusion-polarization; But, more importantly, the "corporate party" that is big-money (dark-money) is controlling public policy by buying elections and influencing voting patterns.

- One of the primary obstacles to societal unity is workplace economic-discrimination. Most Americans know that work is a spiritual commandment from God (the gift of God): no working, no eating (Genesis 3:19). Work is a spiritual obligatory reality with a sacred purpose.

- Eliminate gender discrimination in the workplace and social structure of society: equal pay for equal work.

- We need a dollar that circulates at least three times in underdeveloped and underserved communities as common-sense spiritual solutions for economic justice. Governmental incentives should be given to entrepreneurial investors who are willing to provide goods and services in economically deprived communities (income inequality issues).

- Law enforcement agencies must be transparent in their policies, procedures, and enforcement of violations of laws. No ethnic-category, social class, or religious persuasion of individuals should be profiled by police departments.

State legislatures should enact laws mandating civilian review boards with subpoena power to ensure police-citizen accountability. Police officers are the first line of defense for apprehending law-breakers, and they should never become the judge, jury, and executioner.

Police departments should be very, very concerned about "Stand your ground" laws and the open carry of firearms. These types of laws make community policing more difficult and potentially more unsafe. Body cameras have become a "social justice must" both for the legal protection and civil rights of citizens as well as policemen.

Police officers must be professionally trained in techniques of how to handle family domestic disputes and violence and "emergency" calls.

Police car-chasing incidents have become life and death situations, both for policemen as well as civilians, and therefore, helicopter and drone surveillance should be the first-line of defense used in pursuit of criminals. Community-neighborhood policing is needed to foster better community and police relations (societal stability and social justice). In addition, policemen (citizen policemen) should be given financial incentives to live in the communities/ neighborhoods in which they serve. This will help reduce the fear-factor associated with policing in urban environments.

Sunday morning at eleven o'clock is still the most segregated hour in American society. Why? (Individuals of the same religious persuasion, serving the same invisible God, but cannot worship that spiritual God together in the same physical buildings: It's a choice). This is a monumental spiritual problem. Most of all, churches should model "charity: love and service." Christian churches are speaking "social-truths," but not the kinds of spiritual truths that make individuals free (John 8: 31-32).

"For the leaders of this people cause them to err; and they that are led of them are destroyed. Therefore the Lord shall have no joy in their young men, neither shall have mercy on their fatherless and widows: for every one is a hypocrite and an evildoer, and every mouth speaketh folly. For all this his anger is not turned away, but his hand is stretched out still" (Isaiah 9: 16-17). "For all have sinned, and come short of the glory of God" (Romans 3:23). At one time, we were in some superficial, symbolic respects "one nation under God." Today, America has become a "No-God" society, because too many Americans do not want to spiritually know God. Selah!

12 | An Analysis of Law and Order in America

Individuals have always been in search of themselves rather than God, and individuals in America are no different. As a result, America has become a spiritually troubled nation. Individuals also have the tendency to use God's laws (such as the Ten Commandments) only when it is convenient or benefits their selfish purposes, and that is, to protect them, their trusted loved ones, and personal friends. This kind of "justice" is not blind, but particular. If individuals first spiritually sought God, then justice would indeed be color-blind in law enforcement, sentencing, and hiring practices.

It has been said that the American justice system is the best system of justice in the world. How meaningful is this, when we look at the kind of shape the world is in? "For the wrath of God is revealed from heaven against all ungodliness and unrighteousness of men, who hold the truth in unrighteousness; because that which may be known of God is manifest in them; for God hath showed it unto them. For the invisible things of him from the creation of the world are clearly seen, being understood by the things that are made, even his eternal power and Godhead; so that they are without excuse: because that, when they knew God, they glorified him not as God, neither were thankful; but became vain in their imaginations, and their foolish hearts were darkened" (Romans 1: 18-21).

Ignorance of man's laws (Caesar's laws) is no excuse. But while we know what the purposes of God's laws are, the purposes of Caesar's laws are not quite as clear. It appears as though Caesar's laws are designed solely to protect white males and their property (of course, white females would be considered property). The fatal shooting of Michael Brown by a police officer in Ferguson, Missouri, and the choke-hold death of Eric Garner in New York raise two troubling questions about policing in America:

- What are departmental policies and procedures regarding the use of deadly force against citizens?
- What is the nature of police training as it relates to their role as peace-keepers (rather than killers)?

Based on the evidence, it seems the law simply provides social justification for initiating genocide against black males in the name of law and order as well as keeping other minority groups in check through intimidation and murder. Professional law enforcement training, law enforcement constabularies, and justice according to the law all seem designed to make black males extinct.

The question must be asked: Why do God-fearing, law-abiding individuals allow these blatant miscarriages of equal justice by law enforcement to occur? We can change laws, but the more difficult undertaking is changing the hearts and minds of individuals. Changing the hearts of individuals requires a spiritual transformation. Without a doubt, some men just cannot get over "it"; that is, the spiritual declaration that is contained in the U.S. Constitution: "All men are created equal." To be sure, the moving finger writes on the proverbial wall and then moves on, but the most important thing is to understand the writing on the wall: change the direction or perish.

This genocidal mentality against black males seen in institutional law enforcement must be radically altered for America to survive as a great democratic nation.

Currently, we have sent our military to fight for justice on behalf of individuals who live under repressive foreign regimes. Yet, within our own borders certain repressive voting rights tactics are being employed, repressive law enforcement tactics are perpetuated, and above all, ungodly high unemployment rates in minority communities remain unaddressed.

We are indeed living in perilous, yea, desperate, times. But when Americans stop rejecting God and God's laws and lift up the name of Jesus, God will heal America. "If my people, which are called by my name, shall humble themselves, and pray, and seek my face, and turn from their wicked ways; then will I hear from heaven, and will forgive their sin, and will heal their land" (2 Chronicles 7:14). Of course, there is always a penalty for rejecting common sense, such as the statement uttered by Rodney King: "Can't we all just get along."

13 | Ferguson: The Aftermath

with William Greer, J.D.

The apparent execution-style death of Michael Brown, a young black man, in Ferguson, Missouri, raises alarming concerns about the nature of policing in American society. One question comes to mind: What are the spiritual and sociological implications of the Michael Brown shooting for policing in American society, especially for minority males? An additional concern comes to mind: Why are so many of America's ex-military personnel recruited as police officers? This concern must be addressed because both military and civilian psychiatrists are saying that these individuals are coming home from war experiences with serious mental health issues. Additionally, we must ask why so many police officers as well as ex-military personnel are having family (domestic violence) related problems.

We must do an empirical analysis of how the African-American community in Ferguson both symbolically and literally failed themselves as well as Michael Brown prior to August 9, 2014. It is quite clear to casual observers what the traditional purposes of police organizations have been: protect the property of white males and keep minorities *"checkmated"* through murder and intimidation. Without a doubt, American history is replete with vulgar examples of this "public policy" policing approach against both blacks as well as ethnic white immigrants. When will some white men overcome their disdain for minorities, especially minority males? It has been almost four hundred years of consistent verbal abuse and physical violence without a real "come-by-here-Lord-moment."

Participatory democracy (voting rights/civil rights) is the foundation of a democratic society. Blacks were given these rights in recent times. Unfortunately, the Supreme Court in a recent ruling diluted the Voting Rights Act of 1965. God sees us before we see ourselves. Of course, the after-the-fact awarding of voting rights to blacks is an abomination to God and an insult to the citizenship of Black Americans.

Silence is not golden, it is yellow.

The population of Ferguson is 63 percent black, and yet, in the previous city-wide election, and yet, only 6 percent of the black community voted. Without a doubt, there is no legitimate excuse that can be given for this level of non-participation in the electoral process. This is a travesty against one's self because too many Americans, both black and white, died for the voting rights and civil rights of Americans to use public accommodations and attend the public schools of their choice. For this deplorable state of affairs to exist in the twenty-first century is disgraceful and scandalous. Indeed, this vulgar level of non-democratic engagement is unconscionable.

Voting is a sacred social and moral obligation; therefore, the moral obligation to vote must be reinforced within our families, educational institutions, churches, and civic organizations. Ferguson is a perfect example of the failure of an entire community to protect its children and citizenry, especially in the case of Michael Brown, because he lost his life in a nonsensical confrontation with a police officer. When an entire community is harassed by strangers called police officers because of that community's refusal to participate in the political process, they only have themselves to blame. But, more importantly, this set of circumstances creates an "us versus them" mentality, because the concept of the stranger invariably creates social conflict; therefore, when police officers view an entire community as monolithic, and likewise the community views police officers as monolithic this scenario perpetuates the so-called "blue-code" (us against them mentality). More importantly, traffic-ticket writing becomes a form of taxation without representation to meet a large percentage of the budget for law enforcement. For policing to be effective, it must invariably have a sense of community accountability, that is, community involvement. Blacks in Ferguson were a part of the problem, not the solution to the problem.

If there was a situation of large scale social unrest in American society, would the United States military fire upon U.S. civilians? Without a doubt, order is a necessary social condition for every society. Of course, order is not necessarily justice, but a society must have order before justice can be established. Campus rioting events at Kent State University during the time of the Vietnam War, when a number of unarmed white college students were brutally murdered by the U.S. Military, is a classic example.

I am my brother's keeper. Individual responsibility and collective responsibility are flip sides of the same coin. We cannot have peace in America until individuals universally learn to transcend the color line, that is, rid themselves of the graveyard philosophy of "my way or the highway." Jesus had a plan given to Him by God, and that plan was to die on Calvary to universally redeem the sins of humanity. "Wherefore, as by one man sin entered into the world, and death by sin; and so death passed upon all men, for that all have sinned" (Romans 5:12).

What is the plan of black people, other than the instinct to survive to stay here another day? Again, what is the cultural plan of black people? We know the spiritual plan, but what is the cultural plan of action for insisting that America live up to its solemn creed? Jesus has already died for us, so we do not have to die again but learn to creatively live. However, we should always be willing to die for the sake of righteousness. We humbly submit that our plan of action ought to be to build the Kingdom of God on earth. There is nothing difficult about this, because there is nothing too hard for God. As sociologists, to help individuals transcend the color line intellectually we must be willing to die for righteous principles and godly teaching to live for a righteous cause.

Dr. Martin L. King Jr. said it best in his letter from the Birmingham jail in which he writes about the higher morality and spirituality of self-purification. On the one hand, injustice should not be tolerated in American society. But, on the other hand, those who are the victims of societal injustice should self-purify so as not to participate in their own self-victimization. To be sure, words without deeds are the epitome of immorality. Saying one thing and doing another is not self-purification but self-denigration. In the "shadow of deep disappointment" concerning the race based policies of discrimination in Birmingham, Alabama, at the time, Dr. King wrote about taking direct action in the struggle for basic civil rights:

We had no alternative except to prepare for direct action, whereby we would present our bodies as a means of laying our case before the conscience of the local and national community. Mindful of the difficulties involved, we decided to undertake a process of *self-purification*. We began a series of workshops on nonviolence, and we repeatedly asked ourselves: Are you able to accept blows without retaliating? Are you able to endure the ordeal of jail?

The spirituality of the civil rights movement is laid bare in MLK's letter from the Birmingham jail. The black church, especially in the South, was the hub for the civil rights movement. Black pastors were dedicated spiritual leaders providing guidance for business development, education, and civic and family relationships. Black power and black pride were more than mere slogans. These slogans were attitudes and social behaviors that were transformed into lifestyles. If the black community is to thrive spiritually and economically there must be a rekindling of this spirit.

Recent events in Ferguson exposed a two-fold problem in the black community: internal contradictions and the external legacy of racial bias and institutional racism. At the same time, contemporary civil rights leaders failed to recognize and bring to the conscience of the black community in Ferguson the importance of self-purification as a spiritual-sociological tool for collective survival and community development. Before individuals can hold the purveyors of injustices accountable, they must first engage themselves in a process of self-examination, and if need be, self-purification. Self-purification undergirds the moral superiority of their cause for a just society, just as Dr. King recognized that the moral weight of right is strengthened by moral self-purification. Prior to registering complaints with those external to the community, the community must internally address systemic problems and deficiencies that inflict harm internally upon the community; that is, before holding others responsible for social injustices, individuals must first hold themselves accountable for justice. But, more importantly, blacks must hold themselves accountable for the dollar circulating in the community at least three to four times because this is the only way individuals can become self-sufficient.

As noted earlier, to ensure a more just political and social climate, individuals must participate consistently in the democratic process. Much has been said by politicians, journalists, and purported civil rights leaders about the need for minority constituencies to exercise the franchise (voting rights). However, voter participation includes more than electing political leaders in local communities. Voter registration directly affects the criminal justice system, and moreover, the civic governance of a community as well as society in general. For example, jury pools are convened from voter registration rolls. Civic boards, local policy groups, local land use zoning committees, and ad hoc policy planning and review boards are all in many instances based on voter registration rolls. Of course, this is the only way citizens can hold elected officials accountable. This is not a guess but a statement of fact: if an official is elected with a moderate family income and becomes a multimillionaire you know that there is a dead polecat on the line.

Likewise, sociologically, the upward social mobility of constituent groups within a community is reflective of individuals taking ownership and responsibility for establishing community priorities. When individual members of a particular community take ownership of human development and foster sustainable programs of collective community responsibility for local schools, parks, streets, and youth programming, the community prospers spiritually and economically. Statement of fact: Every individual is accountable for his or her own actions. American leadership has miserably failed black people. We are not becoming better people but bitter people. Where do we go from here? We sincerely hope not to hell in a hand-basket. God does not need everybody; He just needs somebody. Ask Gideon, ask King David, ask Joshua, ask Nathan, ask Abraham Lincoln, ask Lyndon B. Johnson, ask Theodore Roosevelt, ask Martin L. King Jr., and finally, ask Barack Obama. Of course, there are many women who we can ask in the by and by. For example, ask Harriet Tubman, ask Mary McLeod

Bethune, ask Eleanor Roosevelt, ask Florence Nightingale, and finally, ask Madame C.J. Walker. But, above all, let's ask Jesus Christ: "But grow in grace, and in the knowledge of our Lord and Savior Jesus Christ. To him be glory both now and forever" (2 Peter 3:18).

In Politics, Do Things Change or Simply Remain the Same?

14

It has rightly been said: The more things change the more they remain the same. It seems that way in politics. It has been thirty-eight years since James Earl Carter was elected President in 1976. Jimmy Carter was a peanut farmer and the governor of the great sovereign state of Georgia. During the political campaign between James Earl Carter and President Gerald R. Ford, James Earl Carter was typecast as "Jimmy who?" In 2008, the same typecast question was asked: Obama who? That is, Obama was typecast as simply a community organizer. The "elitist establishment" sought to discredit the presidency of

Obama based on occupational mediocrity just as they had sought to discredit Carter. Once elected, the objective was to make Obama a one-term president, just as they had previously done to Carter. Carter was defeated because of liberal Democrats, and Obama was almost defeated because of so-called Blue Dog Democrats. The Senate minority leader, Mitchell McConnell, stated openly the objective of Republicans was to make President Obama a one-term president. President Carter and President Obama are two of the most moral presidents in American history, with the exception of President Obama's advocacy for same-sex-marriage. Both presidents inherited bad socio-economic conditions with one exception: in 2008, America was involved in two unpopular costly wars. Campaign '76, just like campaign 2008, depicted America at a crossroads that called out, "Which way, America?"

To understand the historical context which led to the dilemma of campaign '76, one must understand the impact of President Nixon's victory over Senator George McGovern in 1972. In 1972, Americans overwhelmingly expressed their clear choice. The issues were clear: (1) redistribution of wealth and (2) reorganization of the federal bureaucracy and the dissipation of federal power, especially the notion that government can resolve all societal ills. Senator Barry Goldwater had set the stage for electing Richard Nixon. In 1968 and 1972, the Nixon doctrine of privilege prevailed. The issues were clear: Jimmy Who? versus Jerry What? Again, in 2008, the issues were clear.

Jimmy Carter's campaign raised two overriding concerns: Can religion be effectively used to revitalize American culture and political processes? Attempting to be morally right in politics is a no-no. Second, can blacks and the disinherited poor (the underclass) coupled with the support of socio-economic visionaries alter power arrangements, political institutions, value orientations, and eventually the social system of reward allocation?

While Governor Carter had demonstrated that he was a rational and efficient manager, President Carter's interview in *Playboy* magazine was a profound example of Jimmy Who's comfort-level in his own skin as well as his sense of Christian morality. This was a bit much for the majority population to accept. Carter's style of self-introspection represented culture shock to most White Americans; that is, the ideas and parameters that Carter used to describe the universe and man's place in the scheme of things was foreign and even obsolete to most whites. This is why, despite Carter's southern roots, he had overwhelming support in the Black community. The ideas and features that Carter used to describe the nature of man, God, values, and societal organization made him a different Southerner. Minorities viewed Carter as a moral man. President Carter's ideological concepts were at odds with the institutional structure of American society; this was the basis for the characterization, Jimmy Who? Carter's presidency posed a real threat to America's mind-set. The fear of Whites was expressed in a typical statement: "Well, he won, but he won't be able to do anything." This is precisely the same attitude the "ruling-class" had toward President Obama. What is it that majority Whites fear?

Are Whites afraid ...

- That a positive role of religion in American society might disrupt the status quo? The role of religion has been conveniently compartmentalized, that is, relegated to dealing with matters of "faith," not reason (the separation of church and state doctrine).
- Because Christianity has been prostituted as a means of perpetuating a system of 'privilege

for Whites and a mechanism of social control over minorities? Are some Americans fearful of religion playing a positive role in American society rather than a compartmentalized role? Are they afraid that godly religion would encourage fairness?

In the mid-sixties some elitist Whites announced the death of God and that everything is relative. In twenty-first century America, the death of God in the conscience of many individuals has become a fact of life because society is legalizing sin.

Both Carter and Obama confused the "elitist-image-makers," fair-weather liberals, and cultural conservatives. Both the Carter and Obama administrations were inclusive administrations. This leads us to two questions: (1) Are Americans competent enough to find a spiritual-self amid a materialistic world? (2) Do Americans have the courage to live out the true meaning of the American Creed (Constitution)? We have experienced the "old south" migrated to the "new south called the North," and now, can we stand in a place where there is "no south"? Can we become the United States of America?

Carter's presidency raised some serious questions about institutional-governmental effectiveness and management competence. Similarly, Obama's presidency has raised the same concerns. It is within the power of White elitists to achieve civil rights dignity for all Americans. Far too many Americans have been obsessed with privilege and seeking at the same time to avoid collective responsibility and social cost accountability. Political processes apart from religious processes have brought America to the edge of the moral bankruptcy cliff. In fact, political processes apart from religious processes and spiritual understanding have brought us to national and international disaster.

In 2015, the world knows who James Earl Carter is: peacemaker and the founding spirit of Habitat for Humanity. The world is a better place today because of the work of James Earl Carter as a gentle soul, moral man, peacemaker, and a home builder for the least of those among us. Jimmy Who's simplicity, just like the simplicity of Jesus, is a great example of how we ought to love and serve one another. God gave Noah the rainbow sign; could God be giving us the "climate-sign"? Warm it up; warm it up with love and service for one another.

Politics in the
Best Interest of
Democracy

15

The year 2015 marks the fiftieth anniversary of the passage of the 1965 Voting Rights Act. Voting is a Constitutional right that should never be taken for granted. Let's not just enjoy the theme song "Glory" in the historic movie about Selma, but let's be a participant in voting our conscience for the glory of God. "Vote your conscience and in the morning you shall see the glory of God." Blood was shed and precious lives lost so that all Americans have the sacred privilege of voting. Shame, shame, and more shame on those Americans who fail to exercise the Constitutional privilege of voting in every election. All politics is local; therefore, vote for those candidates who best represent the interests of America. Minorities and fair-minded Whites understand the injustice of some who are hell-bent on preventing minorities from exercising their Constitutional right to vote.

The Scripture below clearly identifies the nature of the spiritual, moral, and political problems that are plaguing America: "For men shall be lovers of their own selves, covetous, boasters, proud, blasphemers, disobedient to parents, unthankful, unholy, without natural affection, trucebreakers, false accusers, incontinent, fierce, despisers of those that are good, traitors, heady, high-minded, lovers of pleasure more than lovers of God; having a form of godliness, but denying the power thereof: from such turn away. For of this sort are they which creep into houses, and lead captive silly women laden with sins, led away with divers lusts, ever learning, and never able to come to the knowledge of the truth" (2 Timothy 3: 2-8). In the past, blacks who were free to vote, voted for Republicans because of President Abraham Lincoln (Emancipation Proclamation). Many whites also voted Republican. The Democratic Party (Dixiecrats) historically was the party of slavery, and the Republican Party was the party of freedom. But, oh, how "Southern Dixiecrats" have jumped ship in the South once again seeking to protect White privilege. The more things change the more they remain the same.

Blacks vote Democratic primarily because of a perceived "big-tent" political philosophy that includes rather than excludes. The Republican Party's political approach to governing perceptually undergirds the notion of White privilege. This is primarily why the Republican Party is ninety-two percent White, and the Democratic Party is over sixty-five percent minority. Pitting one racial/ethnic group against other racial/ethnic groups is not a healthy formula for a harmonious, democratic America. The battle-cry of the present-day Republican Party is Reaganomics: Trickle-down-economics. Their philosophical slogan is, "let's take our country back." I ask the question: Take the country back from whom and for what purpose? When did Whites lose socio-economic-political control over America? Whites still own 90% of all economic assets even though America is browning. Both political party approaches to democratic governance are about power-politics and what is perceived to be in their political party's best interests. Achieving power sharing among diverse racial and ethnic groups in a multi-cultural society is a complicated political process.

What was at one time the old Southern-Dixiecrat Party is now the twenty-first century Republican Party. Southern Dixiecrats (Southern States) blamed the "slaves" (blaming the victim syndrome) and not the Federal Union for their demise during the Civil War. Slaves had no power but to do or die. Even in the year 2015, it seems that way. What happened to the party of Lincoln? How did the party of Lincoln become the party of perceived White Privilege with a Dixiecrat twist? Seemingly, the objective is at any cost find ways to exclude minorities from the electoral process. But, more importantly, this attitudinal political initiative excludes minorities from achieving the American Dream, and, at the same time, blames the victim for everything that is wrong with America (e.g., Welfare).

Poor Whites are political-pawns caught in the middle of something that is beyond their intellectual comprehension because of institutional racism; that is, poor Whites as well as some middle-class Whites are not politically sophisticated enough to understand the strategy of divide and conquer. If they do, they turn a blind-eye to the real cause of their own socio-economic plight. This set of circumstances tends to trivialize the economic contributions of Blacks to the economic success of America as slaves and second-class-citizens (Jim-Crowism). In the twenty-first century after almost 400 years, Blacks are still on the outside of the socio-economic "main-stream" looking in. These facts account for why Blacks remain a separate socio-economic class. However, Blacks must continue to fight the good fight, keep the faith, and God will give the faithful a crown of righteousness.

How do we achieve a just, democratic society? The answer lies in spiritual (Biblical) truths and moral obedience, because obedience is greater than sacrifice, especially when individuals are seeking truth, wisdom, and spiritual understanding. Democracy is for a spiritually enlightened citizenry. "Study to show thyself approved unto God, a workman that needeth not to be ashamed, rightly dividing the word of truth" (2 Timothy 2:15). Obedience is the only foundation for self-development as well as for a healthy democratic society. Let's clearly understand what is currently operating in America in our two-party political system, which in turn, is causing untold political and moral governing confusion, especially in one particular political party (Republican Party). On the other hand, the Democratic Party is "killing America softly" attempting to make sin an issue of civil rights. God is God. Civil rights is not God. God is God all by Himself. All of us know that "... God is not the author of confusion, but of peace, as in all churches of the saints" (1 Corinthians 14:33).

There is a clarion-call blowing in the wind in America: Change direction before it is too late, before God pulls down the curtain, and the sun sets on America. Americans must learn anew how to please God and love and serve each other. The unadulterated disrespect of both the office of the presidency, as well as the man, continues with the election of President Barack Obama. It is an indictment against all that America hoped once to be. When Americans come to themselves, and know the one true God and Jesus Christ whom He has sent, this insanity will be a thing of the past. Selah!

16 Leadership in the Twenty-First Century

Make no mistake about it, "leadership" in the Black community leaves an awful lot to be desired. However, all is not lost. There are new dimensions and promising leadership mentalities on the horizon. Leadership is not about personalities. Leadership is about vision, values, goals, mission, and institutional structures that include, rather than exclude. Of course, this is simply the writer's personal opinion. Therefore, I must quickly add that there are many effective low-profile community-civic leaders and local community-based pastoral leaders who are doing a yeoman job in their respective communities. Self-serving leadership in our major institutions creates dysfunction in the entire community.

Jesus Christ was the greatest leader the world has ever known. He led by example: "If you do not believe me for what I say, then believe me for my works sake." The best way to teach is by example. Every leader should be an example of his/her own teaching: Practice what you teach. A picture is worth a thousand words. Some say that leaders are born. Others say leaders are made (developed). Jesus says: "If any individual desires a position of leadership he/she must first serve." The Black community needs "collectivistic leadership mentalities," not individualistic leadership mentalities. Jesus had a collectivistic leadership mentality based upon the Holy Scriptures of the Jewish tradition. In the twenty-first century, we have the Holy Bible as well as other documents as our basis for leadership development. But, we, as present day humans, write the last chapter. "And this is eternal life, that they may know Thee, the only true God, and Jesus Christ whom Thou hast sent" (John 3:17). Therefore, leadership is a mental, moral, and spiritual endeavor. It has rightly been said: Many are called, but few are chosen.

King Solomon is known as the wisest socio-religious-political leader to have lived. In the book of

Ecclesiastes, Solomon declares: "For wisdom is protection just as money is protection. But the advantage of knowledge is that wisdom preserves the lives of its possessors" (Ecclesiastes 7: 12). Solomon asked God for wisdom, not money. But, God gave him great wealth because he asked for the right thing.

Power manifests itself in two forms: leadership and followership. An individual cannot be the leader of a group of individuals who are not willing to follow where he/she wants to lead. What is leadership anyway? Leadership is a spiritually-moral-collectivistic-mentality that is grounded in conscience.

Politicians should not be referred to as community leaders but should be elected representatives of the expressed collective will of people. Community leadership is of the people, by the people, and above all for the people. Political representation is one of the many serious leadership issues confronting the Black community. Politicians masquerading as community leaders rather than as elected representatives of the will of people is a big problem. Too many Black politicians are representing the interests of the status quo, that is, generally speaking, politicians represent the financial interests of those who finance their campaigns.

Seemingly, the Black community was more prosperous in the era of segregation than it is currently in the so-called era of integration. In the era of segregation we had a more visionary moral leadership mentality based in the Black church experience. The question is, why? In part, the answer lies in the fact that during the era of segregation Blacks were spiritually more grounded because of the quality of moral pastoral religious leadership and our common condition. Today, it seems as though Blacks are hustling backwards because too many blacks spiritually treat other blacks with the same level of disdain as do some whites because of the acquisition of things. Internalizing self-hatred is not a recipe for healthy community development.

Do we want to go back to segregation times, that is, the doctrine of separate but equally-unequal? The answer to the question is a resounding, "Hell no!" But, on the other hand, Blacks cannot operate out of a dog-eat-dog mentality. I got mine, I'm going to get mine, and it's up to you to get your own. Institutional racism is a common condition that affects "all" Blacks, not a particular individual condition. Blacks must come together in spiritual-moral unity, seeking to do the right thing for each other and future generations.

Because we need divine intervention to overcome our socio-economic-political plight, here's where the role of the Black church comes into play. Without a doubt, Black pastoral leadership must be of God, for the Glory of God, and definitely for the spiritual edification of God's people. Is the Christian church going to hell in a hand-basket? If so, what about the world? Unfortunately, in the twenty-first century, name the sin and the Christian church can produce an exhibit.

Finally, leadership is not about hero worship. Some of our leaders do many, many things that are right in the sight of God, but if they do anything against God and the Bible they should be held accountable. God gets the glory. God is the spiritual hero and Jesus Christ is the eternal example. To be sure, leadership is about an institutionalized set of value constructs, principles, and above all a vision for the future that benefits the next generation(s). Selah!

An Analysis of the Political Party System in America

17

Politics in American society has denigrated into an ungodly partisan political power struggle, rather than universal governance oriented toward maximizing the common good. This unfortunate set of circumstances is due to the super-rich and the rich instituting a zero-sum economic game: the super-rich win and the American people lose. This socio-political-economic approach is being fueled because one political party is married to this super-rich philosophical approach and the other political party is engaged to be married. In the final analysis, the *"Corporate Party"* wins and the American people lose. Presently, in American society, roughly two percent of the population received over seventy percent of the nation's increase in wealth since the economic recovery of 2008. Economically, over fifty percent of the American population cannot come up with two thousand dollars in thirty days. Women only earn seventy-seven cents for every dollar men earn; at the same time, in the majority of households in America women are the primary wage earners. These facts suggest that many white voters, especially white males, vote against their own best economic interests. The question is: why?

Both political parties are committing societal adultery, because greed is greed and there are no degrees of greed. This set of political circumstances has created a dysfunctional "major" political party system: Republican Party and Democratic Party. Currently, both major political parties have their moral-political shortcomings. And, of course, the "spiritual" principles of social democracy suffer because of political-governance confusion. Both major political parties to varying degrees are guilty of dividing America in the worst kind of way: dividing families and dividing the rich from the poor. It has rightly been said: "If you did it unto the least of them, you did it unto me"(Matthew 25:40).

Initially, the Republican Party was based upon sound doctrinal governing principles and a common sense "big-tent" approach to governance. As time passed, because of the Civil Rights Act of 1964 and the Voting Rights Act of 1965, the Republican Party began to embrace the political philosophy concerning power, economic advantage, and political electability. Of course, the seed-bed for this political approach was the Goldwater limited government strategy, which culminated itself in Reaganomics. Couple the John Birch Society with Reaganomics and this philosophy made many rural and suburban dwellers feel as though minorities were getting "something for nothing." This is primarily the case because the Republican Party has become primarily a Southern "regional" party. Sadly, the Republican Party is functioning upon a political model that is obsolete. Additionally, President Reagan coined politically emotional phrases to galvanize independent voters, rural and suburban dwellers: "welfare queen, give-away social programs and law and order."

Unfortunately, the current two-party political system has polarized American society and at the same time created social class prejudice, rather than societal spiritual unity. In fact, major political parties have so polarized politics and governance in American society that many Americans now define themselves as "independents," that is, in the middle of nothingness. Sadly, too many politicians are concerned with the next election rather than the next generation. Instead of planning to plant trees they are cutting down trees. Unlike the Republican Party the Democratic Party has a "big tent" progressive political philosophy; and, therefore, can absorb more readily different kinds of political philosophies/factions. To be sure, sometimes this philosophical, political approach creates unbridled factionalism as well.

The Tea Party is an ultra-cultural conservative exclusionary faction of the Republican Party. Seemingly, the primary objective is to hang on the front-door of the Republican Party a subliminal message: whites only, no minorities wanted. This type of messaging physically existed prior to the 1964 Civil Rights Act and the Voting Rights Act of 1965. Living in the past is not a healthy political strategy, nor is this approach a sound societal spiritual unity strategy, because the past was not perfect; it belongs to the devil and the future belongs to God. The present moment belongs to individuals. The Tea Party appears to be anti-fairness and, therefore, more interested in acquiring economic privileges rather than equitable political governance inclusion.

On the other hand, the Republican Party has positioned itself as anti-minority, and the voting numbers tend to bear out this socio-political analysis. Every individual votes in his/her own best self-interest and, therefore, identifies with the political party that advocates their best interest. It appears as though Democratic Party policies are in the best interest of minorities, the nation, as well as the international community. In the past, Republican Party policies were in the best interests of minorities, the nation, and the international community. Seemingly, our European allies are more in agreement with America's current diplomatic approach to international problem solving than the Republican Party, whose approach to resolving international issues appears to be militarism. America should never give comfort to or aid her foes, foreign or domestic.

The Minority Party, because of the hi-jacking of the Republican Party by The Tea Party, has been forced politically into almost wholly aligning itself with the Democratic Party. This, in and of itself, is spiritually, politically, and economically unhealthy for the well-being of the nation. The Minority Party must always be inclusive. Jesus was about inclusion, because all have sinned and come short of the glory of God.

All political parties should be inclusive; that is, it should be of the people, by the people, and for the people. Without a doubt, power for the sake of power is intellectual insanity. To have societal unity and world peace, there must be godly-spiritual purposes associated with the exercise of power. The earth is the Lord's and the fullness thereof; "and it is appointed unto men once to die, but after this the judgment" (Hebrews 9:27). Godly men and women understand this universal "power" principle, therefore, when individuals are faithful over a few things, they will know how to rule (exercise power) over many things. God has spoken to every generation, and His message (theology) from one generation to the next has not changed. Even in the twenty-first century, God is still changing deserts into green pastures and vice versa, therefore, in all that we say and do, it should glorify God and be designed to love and serve each other in the spirit of unity of national purpose and world peace.

What Legacy?

18

These are times in which men in leadership positions refuse to *listen to* and *live by* sound doctrine. It appears that the majority of our political leaders at every level of government are desirous of taking right and making it wrong, and taking wrong and making it right, and making it work. "There is a way which seemeth right unto a man; but the end thereof are the ways of death" (Proverbs 14:12). Of course, we understand that "Fools make a mock at sin: but among the righteous there is favor" (Proverbs 14:9). In the twenty-first century, for understandable spiritual and political reasons, things are not done decently and in order in our governmental system, therefore, the Congressional approval rating is approaching a single-digit figure, because of political governing confusion and political party discord. Unfortunately, most of the governing confusion and societal discord is caused by one political party in particular, because of the personage of the president.

All of this confusion is charged to our children as well as the next generation. Children are a heritage (gift) from God. What is the heritage that's being passed on to our children? Seemingly, the answer is: confusion, confusion, and more confusion. Does America know what God requires of her? "He hath showed thee, O man, what is good: and what doth the Lord require of thee, but to do justly, and to love mercy, and to walk humbly with thy God?" (Micah 6:8). Let's be clear: "Do not be deceived, God is not mocked: for whatever a man sows, this he will also reap" (Galatians 6:7). (If an individual or political party (PP) sows discord, they shall reap discord). Individuals cannot have peace where there is no moral order. Above all, individuals cannot have society and civilization when individuals do not have a conscience.

The press in these United States of America should not *slant* news events one way or the other. There is

"Good News" and the good news is simply this: "The Lord gave the Word: great was the company of those that published it" (Psalm 68:11). The local and national press should thoroughly research issues, and tell the American people the unadulterated truth. Slanting news events and issues creates confusion, social conflict, and societal discord, and above all racial/ethnic tensions. All of us should remember the solemn words of Rodney King: "Can't we all just get along."

Every American desires to have a good name, as the Bible profoundly declares, "A good name is rather to be chosen than great riches, and loving favor rather than silver or gold" (Proverbs 22:1). Of course, President Obama is not an exception to the rule. President Obama's desire is to do well while he can, for as many as he can, and above all how he can. President Obama understands "Every word of God is pure: he is a shield unto them that put their trust in him" (Proverbs 30:5). But, LEGACY is the way the news media portrays Obama's presidency. Most Americans only know the legacy of a few presidents of these United States.

The poet/dramatist, William Shakespeare, wrote five great tragedies. In one of his great tragedies, Julius

Caesar, Shakespeare analyzes Mark Anthony's speech (eulogy). The following quote from Mark Anthony's speech lines up with every American president's term of office: "The evil that men do lives after them; The good is oft interred with their bones." So let it be with Barack Obama. The objective in this editorial is to set the record straight on President Obama's leadership accomplishments, not his legacy. The items listed below are not legacies but are social realities (truths) that have helped many"Americans weather one of the worst economic down-turns in America's history. Legacy is an individual accomplishment. We all know that President Obama does not work in a vacuum. Even though the buck stops at the president's desk there is no "I" in team. Obama's administrative team is made up of many, many dedicated hard working professionals who have accomplished the following:

- Affordable Healthcare Act (Obamacare).
- Saved the banking and automobile industries from total collapse.
- Brought Bin Laden to justice.
- The Lilly Ledbetter Fair Pay Act (Equal pay for women).
- Led the economy through the worst economic crisis since the great depression.

The march for full citizenship for Black Americans has been marred with numerous difficult institutional obstacles. Because of the breakdown of the nuclear family structure, there are too many Blacks losing their spiritual relationship with God as well as losing a leadership vision for a just society. Too many Americans have become idle-minded passengers on a bus that is headed over the moral bankruptcy cliff. The moral walls have been torn down in twenty-first century America. "God standeth in the congregation of the mighty; he judgeth among the gods. How long will ye judge unjustly, and accept the persons of the wicked? Defend the poor and needy: rid them out of the hand of the wicked. They know not, neither will they understand; they walk on in darkness: all the foundations of the earth are out of course" (Psalm 82:1-5).

Lust causes individuals to love that which they should hate. "But, beloved, remember ye the words which were spoken before of the apostles of our Lord Jesus Christ; how that they told you there should be mockers in the last time, who should walk after their own ungodly lusts. These be they who separate themselves, sensual, having not the Spirit" (Jude 1:17-19). "Be not deceived: evil communication corrupt good manners. Awake to righteousness, and sin not;

for some have not the knowledge of God: I speak this to your shame" (1 Corinthians).

What will your life's work say about the glory of God, a future for your children, and above all abundant possibilities for future generations? Selah!

19 | *What Color Is Racism?*

A white male caller on C-SPAN's Washington Journal asked this question: "What color is racism?" The intent of the caller was to create confusion. Racism is not *necessarily* about skin color; even though in America it is about skin color. Universally, racism is about institutionalized power; that is, racism is the powerful ability of an individual or group of individuals, in spite of skin color, to impose their arbitrary will on others even if they resist. Therefore, racism is an institutionalized mind-set. Historically, humankind, in attempts to explain "what is," "what ought to be," and "how what is came to be," created religion as a means of reinforcing their existence.

Some racial groups anthropologically depicted God in their own image (ethnocentrism) to exploit other human beings. The notion of the "stranger" resulted in social myths and belief systems that set the stage for the black and white encounter.

This question must be asked: Do *some* whites hate God? God is the Creator of skin color variety in human beings as well as color in nature (Revelation 4:11). Even in the twenty-first century, the unstated fundamental problem in American society is institutionalized corporate racism. Racism poses some perplexing questions: Why does it exist? What is its social cost? How can it be eradicated? The social pathology of racism invades society like a cancer, spreading moral and spiritual bankruptcy, economic waste, occupational mediocrity, and political polarization and stagnation. The socio-political state of governmental affairs in America is a classic example of the social costs of exclusivism because racism creates a polarized society; therefore, racism is birthed in family structures, nurtured in Christian churches, and intellectually expressed in our educational institutions. Racism in American society is a culturally-based religion, not a God-centered religion, because God hates racism. God created all nations out of one blood. Racism has its mythology (white supremacy), its symbol (physical whiteness), its ideology (the exploitation and dehumanization of non-whites), and it is institutionalized simply because the primary qualification is physical whiteness. The ideological foundation of racism in America is the economic exploitation of non-whites. Currently, there are no racist laws enacted to preclude its existence.

Human societies cannot effectively legislate morality and thought processes. Of course, there are *some* whites who are caught up in the mix of the institutionalizing peer-group immoral mentality. Therefore, racism stems from "idealism and materialism," as manifested in Western socio-religious, philosophical axiology and the rise of the modern capitalist state. In the twenty-first century, given the caste-like economic circumstances of American culture, the color of racism might be green because the American illusion of rags to riches is wishful thinking for some racial and ethnic groups.

Racism in America is about privilege without collective moral responsibility that is restricting access to valued resources based on racial and ethnic origin. At its roots, racism (the economic exploitation of non-whites) is a negative idea, and it includes a series of negative correlates, namely, (1) whites' negative view of themselves, and (2) blacks' negative view of themselves. Racial oppression in American society is a self-filling prophecy. Whites acting as though they are superior and blacks acting as though they are inferior because of the perceived negative consequences associated with acting as equals, which are further complicated by the limited avenues of redress for grievances. When one is seeking to be a free will thinking human being in America, resisting the mandated social norm results in murder in the name of law and order, unemployment, and physical intimidation.

Racism poses five overriding dilemmas: (1) Loss of national purpose; (2) Economic waste; (3) Occupational mediocrity; (4) Political stagnation; and (5) Political confusion. Human economic exploitation and human community are incompatible concepts. Exclusion invariably costs more than inclusion.

There were white English criminals who were given the opportunity to earn their freedom as indentured servants in America. Initially, whites sought to enslave Native Americans, but they refused to succumb to the dehumanization of being a slave and had to suffer the consequence, which was extermination. American and English whites went to Africa in search of slaves and we know the rest of the story because it is American history. Slavery, therefore, became identified with the color black. Blacks, because of the institutional power differential can be prejudiced, but not racist. Without a doubt, the color of institutional racism in America is as white as snow and as white as the corporate power structure. Today, there is a Black family in the White House, and the White House itself is still painted white, it is still called The White House, and the corporate power structure is still overwhelmingly white males.

Racism in its systematic institutional form became pervasive with the rise of mercantilism and capitalism. It eventually became crystallized in the western world to justify the economic exploitation of individuals with "permanent tans." Racism is a white institutional phenomenon simply because too many whites are still in dire need of both personal, peer group influences as well as institutional liberation.

Personal liberation must come first. Whites must culturally "de-whitize" themselves to morally integrate mind and body. By "de-whitize" I mean that whites must give up their current cultural sense of whiteness (white supremacy), not their biological whiteness, to become human. Living beyond physical whiteness is a difficult process because it requires a change of self-concept as well as establishing a system of fairness and consciously living by that system. Living beyond physical whiteness is a difficult process because of peer group influence, meaning, because of scientific and technological advances, whites must give up their "old white ways" and identify with the oppressed and disinherited in the world community. Only then will whites discover the truth about themselves, others, the universe, and above all, God. Modern negative technology (for example, the nuclear bomb) necessitates the nonviolent resolution of conflict. Unless we as Americans change our thought processes and moral codes of behavior, we will forever remain separate and not equal with the social consequences being that of inconsequential spiritual and physical death. So Be It!

Black American History

Black history is more than just the White use of Blacks for slave labor (economic development and European immigration). This essay is not about blaming the victim, but how to take ownership responsibility with limited resources for what was created by a racist institutional system, for after all, Black history begins with a positive "who am I experience"; not hero-worship, because God is the only hero. Who am I? is a spiritual question with an individual as well as an American societal meaning. Black history is about freeing one's self from the inside to the outside. The formula for such a spiritual transformation process is: (a) freedom from fear, (b) faith (God/self), and, (c) tolerance and open-mindedness. Therefore, Black history should be a perpetual living-spiritual process rather than an occasional yearly celebratory experience.

Blacks as a social group have not been able to establish a spiritual-moral affirmation concerning their own human dignity and self-worth because of the dysfunctional-structural nature of Black institutions, namely: families, churches, and educational institutions. By morality, I make reference to an inward process of *spiritual* self-respect dignity, which in turn, stabilizes human relationships. Herein lies the crux of the problem: Black institutions, by and large, give emotional fixes rather than spiritual fixes. This leads one to wonder: When will Blacks move beyond feeling good to learning how to do well?

The twenty-first century demands a new kind of Black consciousness:

- Blacks must acquire the spiritual and moral courage to be black.
- Blacks must acquire the moral-intellectual integrity and courage to restructure their basic institutions: family, church, and educational institutions.

The Black community is experiencing a spiritual-moral crisis of staggering dimensions. Who will save blacks from blacks? Only blacks with God's divine guidance! Without a doubt, only blacks can halt the socio-economic extinction of Black America. The lack of creative intelligence is the source of social disorganization within the Black community as well as in the American society. Spiritual ignorance is the enemy. Witness the evidence:

• Blacks are the only group of individuals who have had "special" institutions, especially built for them, namely, educational institutions (HBCUs). Yet, blacks have not been able to utilize these institutions to free themselves. Why? Replying that whites will not allow us to free ourselves is not a good answer. With God's help Harriet Tubman found a way to free blacks.

• Over forty-two percent of all PhD's granted to blacks are in the field of education. More than seventy percent of all blacks are educated in environments that are 80-100 percent black. Of course, American Blacks are the most Europeanized educated blacks on planet earth; that is, blacks have degrees and keys down to their knees, and *apparently* no Jesus. Where is the common-sense in all this? Yet, at the same time, blacks are the most poorly educated of the poorly educated. Again, I ask: Why? Could it be that there is a positive correlation between degrees and creative intelligence? This is a relevant question because one in five Blacks earn bachelor's degrees from Historically Black Colleges and Universities (HBCUs). This leads one to ask: What are they being taught, and what are we teaching ourselves to become? And, at the same time, black collective survival has decreased proportionally to the number of degrees blacks have earned. Question: Are blacks educating themselves into extinction?

- In 2014, the gross national income of the Black community was 1.1 trillion dollars. Yet, the largest Black owned corporations are entertainment oriented, rather than human development and survival-needs-production oriented. Why does this state of affairs exist? Seeking to have a good time in time, on time, and all the time is not a good strategy for human development, the production of basic survival needs, or community development.

Present educational structures, instructional methods, and ideologies in the Black community militate against creative learning. Existing models of leadership militate against restructuring human thought, spiritual cooperation, and institution building in the Black community. Charity begins at home and then spreads abroad. Of course, this is the only way blacks can effectively "de-whitize" themselves, that is, rid themselves of self-hatred.

Blacks have developed two generations that have become too comfortable in their spiritual ignorance; two generations have been left behind. There is a clarion call blowing in the wind: change directions, because, who needs the poor? is an ethical-moral question. Of course, we need spiritual-moral integration before cultural integration can become a societal reality. Selah!

How to Be a Man to a Man

21

"Let your speech be always with grace, seasoned with salt, that ye may know how ye ought to answer every man" (Colossians: 4:6). My scriptural, sociological training and understanding tells me the social foundation for human interaction between individuals, especially between men, should be formed by this Scripture.

It has rightly been said: Learning how to be a man to another man is far more important than knowing how to be a man to a woman. James Brown said it best: "It's a man's world, but it wouldn't be nothing without a woman, boy or girl." Far too many young men, especially young Black men, are growing up attempting to learn how to be a man to a woman, rather than learning how to be a man to a man. Learning how to be a man to a woman is about sexuality; and, of course, sexuality is a natural process of human nature. Without a doubt, men thinking that they can conquer women through sexuality is simply a losing proposition. Women can look up longer than men can look down. This is why prostitution is a female "thing." I trust that all readers get my drift.

A man must look to the hills from where comes his help and his help comes from God who made Heaven and earth. Learning how to be a man to another man is about moral character, commitment, and intellectual integrity, and this is a learned process (teachable moments). Spiritual communication skills are extremely important in this process. Most Black men have problems communicating with White men because of the institutional racism factor. This unfortunate institutionalized social condition allows White men to formulate stereotyped unhealthy opinions of all Black men. Even though you might have a PhD or No-Degree you are thought of as less than, not equal to the White male species in America. For example, when any Black man approaches a White man, foot-shuffling, scratching his head, and with eyes cast-down, this becomes a stereotypical interaction problem for all Black men.

Allow me to share a personal example. I was attending a Resurrection (Easter-Sunday) service with a prominent Black pastor at a prominent White church. I was responsible for orchestrating the event. The White pastor asked the Black pastor this question: "How did you get a man like Bobby Mills to be with you?" indicating the Black pastor did not know what being a man or pastor was all about. This was a sobering, eye-opening, personal-professional experience for me.

These are especially difficult and troubling times both for America as well as for the Black community. Indeed, the socio-spiritual problems facing the Black community have invariably become "and problems" rather than "either or" problems. Becoming an enemy to one's own self is a real problem. Self is the enemy. Institutional racism is a "White-problem," and of course, Blacks should not make it their problem by internalizing self-hatred. Whites created the racism problem and whites must solve the problem.

Living a significant life is about spiritualism, that is, the fruits of the Spirit (Galatians 5: 22-23). Materialism is about what the world offers. Spiritualism is about God, family, and love and service to others (bearing one another's burdens). Being successful in life and having a successful life requires one to have these spiritual character traits.

Here's the formula for how to be a man to another man despite skin color:

- Have a positive attitude because attitude is life. Attitude determines aptitude, and aptitude determines altitude, that is, how high one will ascend in life.
- Have intellectual integrity based on a firm scriptural belief system. Integrity is about moral integration of flesh and spirit. It is about defending what you believe intellectually, not emotionally and physically.
- Have a word that individuals can count on; that is, say what you mean, and mean what you say. An individual's word must be a commitment. Of course, a man can change his mind because he is not God.
- Have an understanding of physical dress codes as a display of inward intelligence. A man pulls up his pants; walks erect, not only physically, but mentally; dresses without earrings in his

ears. Rebelling against time-honored dress codes is not socially wise.

American culture has become excessively feminized because of the breakdown of the family structure, especially in the Black community. Men thinking and acting out of feminine constructs creates confusion. A man celebrates the truth of what it means to be created in the spiritual image of God when he embraces his manhood realizing that, as a Child of God, he can do all things through a "Righteous Christ," especially when he believes. The battle cry should be: Yes, I can. Yes, I will. Selah.

Workfare versus Welfare

22

Work is God's gift to mankind stemming from Adam's spiritual disobedience in the Garden of Eden. Adam's naming everything in the Garden of Eden was a spiritual work privilege. The excommunication of Adam and Eve from the Garden of Eden brought about a sociological work responsibility: work by the sweat of your brow (sweat equity). Freedom is not free. No work, you do not eat. Adam's listening to the spiritual voice of the devil, rather than the spiritual voice of God within himself, caused all men to have to work by the sweat of their brows and the strength of their minds and bodies. We are to "walk worthy of the Lord unto all pleasing, being fruitful in every good work, and increasing in the knowledge of God" (Colossians 1:10). Work is a sacred responsibility.

For almost four centuries it has suited the economic ends of Europeans to have at their command a large semi-unskilled labor workforce, compelled to work for subsistence wages. To accomplish this goal, European Americans needed a coherent public policy made up of laws (Jim-Crowism), folkways and mores, and diligently planted superiority and inferiority attitudes. In the twenty-first century, by and large, America no longer needs an unskilled-semi-skilled labor workforce. The twenty-first century is the age of technological advances; skilled and technical thinking-oriented labor is required. The methods have changed, but the goal is still the economic exploitation of the masses, especially permanent-tan minorities.

Capitalism is an economic system made up primarily of three basic social classes: upper class, middle class, and lower class (poor). King David said it best: "I have been young, and now am old; yet have I not seen the righteous forsaken, nor his seed begging bread" (Psalm 37:25). The middle class is the buffer-class and the largest social class. As it now stands, we are losing the middle class (the buffer class) because of institutionalized greed. Unfortunately, the middle-class does not mind making socio-economic-political sacrifices to keep the poor, poor by not voting in their own best interests. Do you believe middle-class individuals receive joy from suffering?

To perpetuate this coherent public policy of economic exploitation of minorities (haves-versus-have-nots), it required the participation of governments (federal, state, and local), churches, schools, the press, and society at large. Everyone has some "skin" in the exploitation of the masses economic game. Even the economic exploiters are being exploited spiritually; they just do not realize the nature of the spiritual consequences. "It is easier for a camel to go through the eye of a needle, than for a rich man to enter into the kingdom of heaven" (Matthew 19:24). What has gotten us in this horrible mess is the same thing that can get us out of this socio-spiritual predicament, and that is, if America has the spiritual will to do so.

The middle-class must spiritually answer the Cain question: "Am I my brother's keeper?" (Genesis 4:9). The lower classes must have enough faith to believe that this too shall pass: "But without faith it is impossible to please him: for he that cometh to God must believe that he is, and that he is a rewarder of them that diligently seek him" (Hebrew 11:6). "But if we hope for that we see not, then do we with patience wait for it" (Romans 8:25).

The United States of America is the most intellectually sophisticated technological society on planet earth, therefore, after 395 years as a multicultural society, we should be able to call timeout on the economic exploitation of the masses. America includes spiritually, philosophically, and doctrinally, but excludes economically. This is why the definition of full employment is not zero unemployment, but 3-4 percent of the potential majority workforce unemployed.

The welfare system was created as a safe-guard (safety-net for the lack of jobs) for the majority population so as to contain uprisings against the structural economic inequities fostered by the ruling class establishment. On the one hand, the image of welfare is given to permanent-tan minorities; on the other hand, the reality is that there are more majority Americans on welfare than minorities. In terms of population percentages, however, because of lack of job opportunities there are more minorities on welfare. There has never been a job for every American who is willing to work. The question is: Why does this economic condition exist in America? The answer is:

Partisan politics. Of course, there are many other contributing factors, but bottom-line politics (institutionalized greed) is the primary economic factor; that is, "too big to fail," and sending jobs abroad for cheap labor (vulgar profiteering).

Until Americans grow spiritually and introspectively, and clearly understand the full meaning of the Scripture cited below, we will continue to be a nation of the "haves-versus-have nots," which will perpetuate a dog-eat-dog mentality producing a country divided against itself. "Bear ye one another's burdens, and so fulfill the law of Christ. For if a man think himself to be something, when he is nothing, he deceiveth himself. But let every man prove his own work, and then shall he have rejoicing in himself alone, and not in another. For every man shall bear his own burden" (Galatians 6:2-5).

Without a doubt, historically, the economic playing field has never been level for all Americans. Allow me to paraphrase Psalm 1:1-6: 'A righteous nation does not walk in the counsel of the ungodly, nor stand in the way of sinners, nor sit in the seat of the scornful. But, a righteous nation delights in the law of God, because the law of God is love, service and freedom. Happy is the nation that keeps God's law of love.'

147

Allow me once again to paraphrase Psalm 20:7: 'Some trust in war, and some trust in peace, but every American should place his/her trust in God.' Selah!

Selma

23

Selma is a historical documentary about American history; it is not just another movie. It is a documentary that every American should see, especially White Americans. It's mind-boggling that the 87th Academy Award Nomination Committee disrespected the movie *Selma*. At last, Hollywood has shown its true colors and demonstrated to the world that they cater to whiteness. The Academy Committee lacks moral-intellectual integrity because Hollywood does not honor talent and creativity but whiteness. Now the world knows who Hollywood is because of the snubbing of the movie *Selma*. It is a sad day in American society when a documentary film of this historic magnitude is not recognized for its epic contributions to the Civil Rights Movement. *Selma* has everything individuals love in a movie: drama, suspense, intrigue, mayhem, and violence in all of its raw, racist ugliness.

Twenty-first century America has a Black president and he cannot protect the Civil Rights legislation that President Johnson signed in 1964 and the Voting Rights Act passed in 1965 because of political partisan polarization (Congress and Supreme Court). For ungodly reasons, the Supreme Court recently stripped the 1965 Voting Rights Act of key provisions.

"For the time will come when they will not endure sound doctrine; but after their own lusts shall heap to themselves teachers, having itching ears; and they shall turn away their ears from the truth, and shall be turned unto fables" (2 Timothy 4:3). The right to vote is the very foundation of American democracy, and, of course, the U.S. Constitution guarantees it. Yet, history tells a different story about voting rights for Blacks in America: they have never been "free" to vote without it tainted with malice in "the land of the free and the home of the brave."

Make no mistake about it, I am not a professional

movie critic, but *Selma* refueled and triggered memories from my theological training. In 1964, I was a young seminarian at Colgate Rochester Crozer Divinity School (CRCDS) in Rochester, New York. Two weeks before the scheduled Selma march, the seminary invited Malcolm X as a guest lecturer to an annual convocation event. At that time, there were only twenty Black seminarians enrolled in CRCDS. I can vividly recall listening to Malcolm X speak the truth about race relations in America. I was in awe listening to Malcolm X as he evoked tears of God-fearing redemption from both whites and blacks at a predominantly White seminary. After hearing Malcolm X's speech and watching the media continuously play the horrific images of violence heaped on the bodies of Americans seeking their constitutionally declared voting rights, my classmates and I felt it was time we joined the movement. My fellow Black classmates, Wilson Fallin, Bobby Joe Saucer, Archie Allen, Edward Jackson, and I jumped in our car and headed to Selma. We remained in Selma for a few days, waiting with expectation to take part in this historic event only to have the march canceled. Due to the unexpected cancellation, we had no other choice but to return to CRCDS. The march from Selma to Montgomery took place three months later.

Without a doubt, any God-fearing American who views this documentary cannot sit through the movie without shedding tears. I cried many times. Viewing *Selma* reiterates to all Americans, especially Black Americans who do not exercise their constitutional right to vote, that they do a disservice not only to themselves, but also to those individuals who suffered life-threatening injuries as well as those who died for the right of all Americans to vote. The U.S. Constitution is an almost perfectly written document. It is a document the world has not seen before; not even the Magna Carta included everyone. However, the legal enforcement of the document is mired in race and ethnicity, social class and gender discrimination.

In the twenty-first century, Blacks must also understand the cause and effect mirrored in the results of their own behavior concerning their socio-economic plight. *Selma* clearly demonstrates that the behavior of some Whites has been notoriously ungodly over the almost four hundred years that Blacks have been in America. They have set a distorted example of Christianity for the world because God hates racism. Hollywood just set a bad example. Of course, this is why we still have institutional racism in the twenty-first century; some whites in high places set bad examples for others. We may not have racism by law, but racism still exists in individual mindsets and institutional power sources. Shame, shame, and more shame on Hollywood elites.

Allow me to paraphrase the Weeping Prophet Jeremiah: "Oh that my head were waters, and mine eyes a fountain of tears, that I might weep day and night for [Hollywood]." (Jeremiah 9: 1) So where is there hope for the perilous plight Black Americans face even after 400 years of contempt? To conclude the matter, I leave this Scripture for all God-fearing Americans to ponder: "What then shall we say to these things? If God is for us, who is against us?" (Romans 8:31). So be it.

A Letter to the U.S. Supreme Court

24

American society is founded upon an enlightened, spiritual, human rights-principled declaration: "We hold these truths to be self-evident that all men are created equal, that they are endowed by their creator with certain inalienable rights, and among these are life, liberty and the pursuit of happiness." The U.S. Constitution is almost a perfectly written governing document. It is a document that the world had never seen before, and probably will not see again, because it theoretically included everyone as equal members of society, and, as stated before, the Magna Carta does not include everyone. Europeans and people of other countries left their countries of origin, landing on American soil, searching for religious freedom and economic opportunity. Even with such an almost perfectly written document, the legal enforcement of the document is mired in race, ethnicity, social class, "States Rights," and gender discrimination. Unfortunately, Constitutional framers could not live by the tenets of the magnificent document that they had written.

The initial conceptual basis for the principle of "States' Rights" was the preservation of some independent sense of States' Rights. Southern States used the principle of States' Rights to preserve and perpetuate the institution of slavery. This was a monumental error in moral judgment because it allowed State sovereignty to trump Federal centralized authority in other areas as well. This error in judgment allowed State and Federal lines of authority over time to become blurred. It is my sincere hope that history does not repeat itself. The majority of Americans profess to live by Christian doctrines and spiritual principles. Let's not make the same fatal mistake again by skirting the moral and spiritual issues involved in the so-called same-sexmarriage debate.

Homosexuals, adulterers, and fornicators all have the human right based upon free will (choice) to be intimate with other consenting adults in the privacy of their homes or behind any closed doors. Sin is about free will (choices), not birth conditions. God is not schizophrenic. "Let this mind be in you, which was also in Christ Jesus" (Philippians 2:5).

In a few months, the Supreme Court will decide the so-called civil rights issue of same-sex marriage, which in turn, would give legal civil rights status to sexual intimacy between men and men and women and women. A strange turn of non-enlightened events!

Homosexuality is a covenant with death, and therefore, engenders a culture of death. Glorifying death in either its real or symbolic dimension is an unwise proposition. Life is about life, that is, how individuals live and the choices they make in the "dash" between birth and death. Again, life is not about death.

All sins are against the spiritual commandments of God. Simply put, homosexuality is against the spiritual command of God: "Be fruitful, and multiply, and replenish the earth, and subdue it" (Genesis 1:28). Two males cannot fulfill God's spiritual command; likewise, two females cannot fulfill God's spiritual command. In reality, there is no such thing as same-sex marriage spiritually and morally. While some States have legalized this insane public policy approach to family life for socio-economic-political reasons and family-related pressures, it is still an insane approach to nation-building (society). Marriage is between a man and a woman because of the reality of procreation (a covenant with life). The bottom line in marriage is procreation (children), the development of children, and the protection and nurturing of children in a spiritually wholesome environment. The bottom line in homosexuality is death. This is precisely why Sarah, the wife of Abraham, the father of faith, beseeched God to give her children, "or else I die." At the center of the concept of marriage is God's spiritual command concerning procreation. This is precisely why God created human beings spiritually in his image: male and female (Genesis 1:27).

Obedience is greater than sacrifice, especially when we seek the truth. Obedience is the foundation of the Christian experience. All of us should be truth-seekers, not lie-accommodators, especially those in "high governmental places." Because of choice, homosexuality is a big, big lie. Let's not lead people astray. The decision is as simplistic as this document. Let's not make this a complicated matter based upon the choice imperfections of human beings. All of us should hold this precious truth: "Lay hands suddenly on no man, neither be a partaker of other men's sins: keep thyself pure" (1 Timothy 5:22). This Scripture ought to be an important legal consideration in such an important societal-structurally altering decision as legalizing same-sex-marriage. Society begins in the family between a man and a woman.

We are marching toward a moral bankruptcy cliff where all reprobate minds ultimately end-up, and that is, spiritually dead. Physical death is inevitable. Individuals have no choice whatsoever in this matter. Since an individual is going to die anyway, even suicide is not a real choice (just keep on living). "But she that liveth in pleasure is dead while she liveth." She in this Biblical context refers to both sexes.

For almost four hundred years, we have based our civil discourse and civil laws upon our professed knowledge of the Law Giver and the Ten Commandments: "Where there is no vision the people perish: but he that keepeth the law, happy is he" (Proverbs 29:18). I pray to almighty God that individual members of this august body will have the intellectual, moral integrity to vote their conscience. "God judgeth the righteous, and God is angry with the wicked every day" (Psalm 7:11). Lest we forget:

"For He saith, I have heard thee in a time accepted, and in the day of salvation have I succoured thee: behold, now is the accepted time; behold, now is the day of salvation." (2 Corinthians 6:2). God gave Noah the rainbow sign as a promise after the destruction of a decadent society that He would never use a flood again. No more water, but fire next time. Selah!

God is God: Civil Rights Is Not God

25

Let's not be stupid. If it is against God, it is against mankind. "For the wrath of God is revealed from heaven against all ungodliness and unrighteousness of men, who hold the truth in unrighteousness …" (Romans 1:18). Even American society has codified in its civil codes of law the phrase "that ignorance of the law is no excuse." It is clearly stated within the pages of God's instruction manual: "Because that which is known about God is evident within them; for God hath showed it unto them. For the invisible things of him from the creation of the world are clearly seen, being understood by the things that are made, even his eternal power and Godhead; so that they are without excuse ..." (Romans 1:19-20) We know that sins committed by both heterosexuals and homosexuals that are against the Word of God are condemned by God. Of course, "All scripture is given by the inspiration of God, and is profitable for doctrine, for reproof, for correction, for instruction in righteousness ..." (2 Timothy 3: 16).

Individuals sin against God because they do not retain God in their hearts and minds (conscience). "Thy word have I hid in mine heart, that I might not sin against thee" (Psalm 119: 11). When heterosexuals and homosexuals repeatedly commit the same sins over and over, God turns them over to a reprobate mind because it becomes a problem of indwelling sinful choices. "And even as they did not like to retain God in their knowledge, God gave them over to a reprobate mind, to those things which are not convenient; being filled with all unrighteousness, fornication, wickedness, covetousness, maliciousness; full of envy, murder, debate, deceit, malignity; whispers, backbiters, haters of God, despiteful, proud, boasters, inventors of evil things, disobedient to parents, without understandings, covenant-breakers, without natural affection, implacable, unmerciful: who knowing the judgment of God, that they which commit such things are worthy of death, not only do the same, but have pleasure in them that do them" (Romans 1:28-32).

"God judgeth the righteous, and God is angry with the wicked every day" (Psalm 7:11). Too many individuals in American society think they have more wisdom and common sense than God. "When they knew God, they glorified him not as God, neither were thankful; but became vain in their imaginations, and their foolish hearts were darkened. Professing themselves to be wise, they became fools ..." (Romans 1:21-22). God is not confused. When each individual is conceived in their mother's womb, God knows about it, even down to the number of hairs on your head. Individuals might become confused as a result of the dictates of their family structures, churches, educational institutions, peer group, and environmental influences. "For, God is not the author of confusion, but of peace, as in all of the churches of the saints" (I Corinthians 14:33). "Therefore being justified by faith, we have peace with God through our Lord Jesus Christ" (Romans 5:1).

Men engaging in sexual acts with other men and women engaging in sexual acts with other women is strictly about maximizing the pleasure principle, not about being fruitful and multiplying (Genesis 1:27-

28). We should love each other as commanded by God, but not to the extent of having intimate sexual relations with the same sex. "But she that liveth in pleasure is dead while she lives" (1 Timothy 5:6). She, in this Biblical context, refers to both females as well as males. All sins are choices, not birth conditions based upon God and nature. Sin always ushers in spiritual death and sometimes even physical death. "For the wages of sin is death; but the gift of God is eternal life through Jesus Christ our Lord" (Romans 6:23). When individuals seek to subvert God's will, it is always a losing proposition. When men and women deliberately attempt to subvert God's will and slap nature in the face, it is indeed a losing proposition. Sodom and Gomorrah teach us this profound lesson.

A God-fearing society should not embrace same-sex-marriage simply because society begins and ends with the family. No individual is born through same-sex marriage. So goes the family, so goes society as well as the world. Parents of homosexual children should love their children, but at the same time should not ask society to take on the sins of their children. This is why God warns us: "Lay hands suddenly on no man, neither be partaker of other men's sins: keep thyself pure" (1 Timothy 5:22). Parents have a spiritual-moral obligation to teach their children about sexuality and gender identification (role-playing). For example, individuals are born either male or female. Male and female are the statuses. Gender role identification is based upon socialization and environment. Consequently, a male can choose to be a man or a homosexual. A female can choose to be a woman or a lesbian. Mental temperament is not defined by sex-status (biology), but by family socialization and environmental socialization into a culture (economic responsibility). Sexuality is the "gut" and creative impulse of a community and civilized society. When sexuality is "thingified" and commercialized solely for pleasure, environmental quality of life declines and society begins to decay morally. Life is not a "freebie," and least of all is sexuality. The story of Adam and Eve teaches this profound lesson.

American society has enough laws enacted in civil and criminal codes to protect the civil rights and civil liberties of every citizen, therefore, we do not need to enact new laws to promote and legalize sin. All sins are individual choices. What goes on behind closed doors should remain behind closed doors, whether it's homosexuality or heterosexuality.

Attempting to subvert the Word of God is always a

dangerous proposition. Individuals are waxing cold and refuse to listen to sound doctrine. God is not fooled or mocked; individuals reap what they sow. Vanity always creates societal chaos. America needs a national symbol of hope and collective integrity. Can American families, Christian churches, and educational institutions provide such a leadership symbol? Selah!

26 Eternal Questions

Since the beginning of time, human beings have asked certain eternal questions, especially questions concerning the existence of God, and what is ultimately expected of human beings in life. Every individual must draw a circle around self so he or she can understand life. This helps us to understand God, because every individual must come to know God for himself. More importantly, individuals will know what to include in their circle of life and what to exclude. As a flawed "graveyard traveling" human being with many fallibilities, I was born in the South to a family with meager economic resources, yet, by the grace of almighty God, I was the second Black individual to obtain a PhD in the field of sociology from Syracuse University. In my parents' home and my grandparents' homes it was always taught: "In this family, we will serve the LORD"; and, of course, "I was glad when they said unto me let us go into the House of the Lord." Without a doubt, my life experiences have unequivocally taught me to know that there is a God!

Listed below are some eternal questions that human beings have asked from the beginning of time:

- Is there a God?
- What is the meaning of life?
- Is there predestination?
- Is there life-after-death?

Even with my limited spiritual knowledge and understanding of God, these are eternal questions that no individual can absolutely know, and of course, we do not need to absolutely know. If an individual did know the absolute answer to these questions then he/she would be as "GOD." If we did, we would be God. Individuals can only know in part, because faith must be the cornerstone of our knowing and understanding. "But without faith it is impossible to please him: for he that cometh to God must believe that he is a rewarder of them that diligently seek him" (Hebrews 11:6). The earthly connection between our faith and spiritual understanding is through reading the Holy Bible: "But grow in grace, and in the knowledge of our Lord and Savior Jesus Christ. To him be glory both now and forever. Amen" (2 Peter 3:18).

Human social behavioral patterns are conditioned by family structures, institutional churches, and educational institutions with many "strange and secular contestable variables" in-between. Of course, the unpredictable circumstances of human nature make life no crystal staircase; there are thorns and thistles everywhere.

Our educational and religious institutions ought to work together reinforcing, enhancing, and edifying human thought processes that go together like hand and glove. In too many instances, pastoral leaders declare that an educated individual and spirituality do not integrate well in any social-spiritual-institutional environment. (The reason being many pastoral leaders are not educated in the Biblical procedures of church polity.) "So then faith cometh by hearing, and hearing by the word of God" (Romans 10:17). The following Scripture is precisely why education and Christianity go hand and hand: "Blessed is he that readeth…" (Revelation 1: 3). Allow me to paraphrase: "Hide God's word in the heart of your mind so that you might not sin against God" (Psalm 119: 11).

How do we achieve Jesus' declaration that earth and Heaven can be on one accord when we do the "will of God"? Obviously, the only way earth and Heaven can become one is by "hearing the Word of God, reading the Bible with spiritual clarity, and growing in grace and the knowledge of our Lord and Savior Jesus Christ." Of course, individuals must spiritually desire understanding of the following Scripture: "Sanctify them through thy truth: thy word is truth" (John 17:17).

God says He knew you before you were conceived in your mother's womb (your Garden of Eden), but that's God. With human beings, life begins in the family structure between a man and a woman (married or un-married), not same-sex. Society begins in the family context.

All Americans must clearly understand this Scripture: "For God is not the author of confusion, but of peace, as in all churches of the saints" (1 Corinthians 14:33) Therefore, our earthly question is: How do we live in peace and harmony both spiritually and materially within our three basic institutions: family, church, and education?

What will help Americans learn how to effectively deal with eternal questions is enumerated below:

- American family units must re-orient themselves toward spiritualism rather than materialism, because family is a spiritual unit, not an economic unit. Money and income do not satisfy "lovers of money"; but there is great gain in godliness with spiritual contentment. Individuals who love money will never be satisfied with money. Individuals come into the world with nothing, and your "family" will not allow you to take anything out.
- Institutional Christianity (local churches) must foster stewardship, and train and develop godly pastoral leaders rather than promote celebrity-style-worldly-preacher-vanity.
- Educational institutions must foster creative learning processes by teaching individuals how to think spiritually, not how to obtain a degree without having spiritual common-sense.

God desires that all individuals come to a spiritual

understanding in life whereby they can say unequivocally, "Yes, LORD, not my will, but thy will be done." I have not thoroughly answered these eternal questions, not even for myself, but I trust that I have shed some spiritual light on these eternal questions in the context of being an earthly dweller with a heavenly mind. Lest we forget: "God judgeth the righteous, and God is angry with the wicked every day" (Psalm 7:11). To be sure, individuals cannot throw bricks and at the same time hide their hands, because your sins will find you out. Selah!

Beau Biden: Faithful to God, Self, Family, and Country

27

Life consists of swift transitions, and without a doubt, life is not about extremes, but the in-betweens. How we live is the ultimate question. Hence, life is about the quality of the "dash" between birth and death (womb and tomb). I did not personally know Beau Biden or other members of Beau Biden's nuclear family and extended family; but, I do know Vice President Biden, because of his high profile statesman position, and, I did watch the spirit-filled home-going ceremony for his son, Beau, on MSNBC.

Some readers might ask the question, why an editorial on Beau Biden, an individual the writer did not personally know? Here's why: I was in spiritual awe as I listened to the President of the United States, a friend of the Biden family, filled with God-fearing emotion, spiritually eulogize the life of Beau Biden. President Obama spoke of Beau Biden in a loving and brotherly manner. The president spoke of Beau Biden's love and service to others, devotion to family and friends, and military service to his country. Some say it takes a village, but I say it takes a country such as the United States of America to raise an individual such as Beau Biden. And, of course, I said to myself: "Beau Biden was a God-fearing spiritual man, loved by other God-fearing Americans; but, more importantly, his funeral displayed America coming together as 'One Nation under God.'" It is imperative that we are able to embrace each other during times such as this, and demonstrate a unified love and appreciation for a life well-lived. I was spiritually motivated to research the life of Beau Biden.

Parenthetically, I must comment on the environmental conditions. I observed a local church (parish) community and the State of Delaware conduct sacred civic affairs in an orderly and decent manner. The Bible states: "Let all things be done decently and in order" (1 Corinthians 14: 40).

There are very few European Americans who have impressed me spiritually, or who I have been exposed to through the mass-media, yet, I can truly say that this writer experienced a spiritually uplifting moment watching the home-going service of Beau Biden. As Americans, we should aspire to inspire before we expire. Such was the life of Beau Biden. As Christians, we are expected to try the spirit by the spirit. We are commanded to love and serve each other because Jesus first loved us. Without a doubt, Vice President Biden's statesman-like behavior and moral character was thoroughly ingrained in the moral fiber of his son. Righteousness does not have a color because it is of the Spirit of God.

Every individual has two temples within their being: spiritual and flesh. "And what agreement hath the temple of God with idols? For ye are the temple of the living God; as God has said, I will dwell in them, and walk in them; and I will be their God, and they shall be my people. Wherefore come out from among them, and be separate, saith the Lord, and touch not the unclean thing; and I will receive you, and will be a Father unto you, and ye shall be my sons and daughters, saith the Lord Almighty" (2 Corinthians 6:16-18).

From all human indications, Beau Biden developed the spiritual temple of God in his heart and mind rather than living by the flesh. "What? know ye not that your body is the temple of the Holy Ghost which is in you, which ye have of God, and ye are not your own? For ye are bought with a price: therefore glorify God in your body, and in your spirit, which are God's" (1 Corinthians 6:19-20). It appears to this casual observer that Beau Biden listened to and cultivated the Spirit of God in making decisions throughout his life. He turned down the opportunity to be appointed senator of the state of Delaware, because he understood this Scripture: "Be careful for nothing; but in everything by prayer and supplication with thanksgiving let your requests be made known unto God. And the peace of God, which passeth all understanding, shall keep your hearts and minds through Christ Jesus" (Philippians 4: 6-7). Beau Biden asked Almighty God for permission to use his body and spirit in helping to establish a more perfect union by being a peacemaker, not a politician.

Beau Biden was an outstanding leader in his local community, and now he is a memorable son, husband, father, and an all-American public servant. No individual can live and not experience death. All Americans should ask this profound question: "O death, where is thy sting? O grave, where is thy victory? The sting of death is sin; and the strength of sin is the law. But thanks be to God, which giveth us the victory through our Lord Jesus Christ" (1 Corinthians 15:55-57).

The individual spiritual consciousness of physical death is what helps us understand morality (God), not situational-morality and situation-ethics. The Gospel writer Paul said it best: "For I am now ready to be offered, and the time of my departure is at hand. I have fought a good fight, I have finished my course, I have kept the faith: henceforth there is laid up for me a crown of righteousness, which the Lord, the righteous judge, shall give me at that day: and not to me only, but unto all of them also that love his appearing" (2 Timothy 4:6-8).

Based upon my limited spiritual understanding of Beau Biden's life journey, I sincerely believe he accepted the call of Christ to love his brother as he loves himself. He spiritually understood Saint Paul's testimony, because he did not turn his back on God, family, and country. Even though Beau Biden was a lawyer, he clearly understood that the law of God is superior to the law of man. I sincerely believe that he did not blaspheme against the Spirit; his life is a testimony to that. Spiritual growth and spiritual maturity have no time frame. Selah!

God-made versus Man-made

28

Only God can form a woman from a man, and only God can make a man (Genesis 2:1-25). God's work is performed in light of eternity; it is not conditioned by time and space. A man can make a thing and men can make material things, but only God Almighty brings forth a woman from a man. Without a doubt, out of confusion comes more confusion. Christians and spiritual-minded individuals should not be confused, but confused secularists-humanists can confuse innocent children.

A man has nothing whatsoever to do with the making of a woman. Generically, the concept woman literally means (one-man) with two sex-statuses: male and female. The male specie has a penis and the female specie has a womb; therefore, it is a womb that makes (defines) a woman as a woman, not mental illusions of grandeur. Symbolically, the woman's womb is the same as the Garden of Eden, because when a child is conceived it develops in the mother's womb for nine months. It is a fertile life-giving sanctuary for human development as was the Garden of Eden. When any man arrogantly thinks that he can make or become a woman, God is not pleased. God created a woman (Eve), and gave Adam (man) the privilege of naming her, not to be her God, but to be her covering (help-mate) from the spiritual wiles of the devil. When a man seeks to be a woman's god, sociologically it is called male chauvinism, and playing God is called having a God-complex. Without a doubt, playing God is not the same as being God, because playing God is dangerous to your spiritual well-being.

"For the wrath of God is revealed from heaven against all ungodliness and unrighteousness of men, who hold the truth in unrighteousness; because that which may be known of God is manifest in them. For the invisible things of him from the creation of the world are clearly seen, being understood by the things that are made, even his eternal power and Godhead; so that they are without excuse: because that, when they knew God, they glorified him not as God, neither were thankful; but became vain in their imaginations, and their foolish heart was darkened. Professing themselves to be wise, they became fools, and changed the glory of the uncorruptible God into an image made like corruptible man, and to birds, and four-footed beasts, and creeping things. Wherefore God also gave them up to uncleanness, through the lusts of their own hearts, to dishonor their own bodies between themselves: who changed the truth of God into a lie, and served the creature more than the Creator, who is blessed forever. Amen" (Romans 1: 18-25).

When individuals arrogantly think that they can determine their own sex-status, it is an idolatrous, vain attempt at equalizing one's self to God; it is idolatry of the most vulgar blasphemous kind and spiritual form. God is definitely not pleased. "God judgeth the righteous, and God is angry with the wicked every day" (Psalm 7:11). Secularism is not God. Sexuality is not God. Civil rights is not God. Humanism is not God. And, to be sure, vanity is not God. God is God all by Himself. He does not need any help being God.

In 1976, *Newsweek* magazine published a research study identifying the ten things American men feared the most. Topping the list was fear of being poor (lack of money). In position number seven was fear of latent homosexuality tendencies: no more. We can assume that the fear of homosexuality was based upon fear of sin, because as graveyard travelers, individuals definitely ought to fear sin, because one day all persons must spiritually give an account to God for deeds done in the flesh. But, of course, "Fools make a mock at sin: but among the righteous there is favor" (Proverbs 14:9).

Glorifying ignorance of God is not a societal occasion for glorifying and celebrating fool-heartedness. Double shame on *Vanity Fair* magazine for spiritually disrespecting and morally dishonoring the spiritual and divine meaning of womanhood, and above all, confusing America's children concerning sex-status identity; that is, attempting to change the will of God in a human being, physically, mentally, and morally – an abomination makeover. Children are a heritage from God and should not be destroyed for lack of knowledge of God. Portraying this person on the front-cover of a magazine that was established to dignify the spiritual femininity of women and their biological role as mothers is to display the least despicable "male chauvinism," that is, vain male-arrogance. Christian God-fearing women ought to be disgusted to the nth degree at the insult hurled at them by *Vanity Fair* magazine. The spiritual trinity (God the Father, Son, and Holy Spirit) should be glorified, not the worldly trinity of theology, sociology, and psychology. America is in a spiritual-moral dilemma because Christians and spiritual-minded individuals refuse to speak up and speak out against the immoral insanity of those who are attempting to play God. Silence is not golden, but consent.

This is the moral question that Christian women and spiritual-minded women need to ask *Vanity Fair*. Why don't you show us the "womb," not the face? Show us the "womb" where life can be conceived, made fruitful, and multiplied! Save the children is the battle cry.

God gave us a real world. Ungodly men have created an unreal world made up of phony arbitrary realities. My earnest prayer to the Christian women and spiritual-minded women of America is simply this: don't become idle-minded participants in tom-foolery! That is, cover your children with godly motherly love so that they might grow to understand: "When I was a child, I understood as a child, I thought as a child: but when I became a man, I put away childish things. For now we see through a glass, darkly, but then face to face: now I know in part; but then shall I know even as also am I known" (1 Corinthians 13:11-12).

God gave Noah the rainbow sign: no more water, the fire next time. Pulling the moral walls down is a dangerous societal proposition. Behold the likes of Sodom and Gomorrah, the Greek Empire, and the Roman Empire. Get ready America! The time is at hand for "Blessed is he that readeth, and they that hear the words of this prophecy, and keep those things which are written therein: for the time is at hand" (Revelation 1:3). Selah!

29 Betrayal and Hypocrisy

American society is built upon a political survival strategy that is undergirded by democratic principles and socio-political-economic processes. We all know that the preamble to the Constitution and the Declaration of Independence was built upon spiritual-political truisms. The U.S. Constitution is an almost perfectly written document. Unfortunately, the founders could not live up to the spiritual sacredness of the creed, that is, the moral backbone of the document. Even now in the twenty-first century, Americans are unable to embrace the spiritual reality that "all men are created equal, and endowed by their creator with certain inalienable rights." Let's examine the socio-political-economic nature of the spiritual betrayal and hypocrisy that is running rampant in American society, especially in Texas.

Leadership betrayal and hypocrisy have become pervasive socio-political-economic problems in American culture, not because of a lack of economic resources, but because of the lack of spiritual-moral will. Without a doubt, God sees us before we see ourselves. When individuals practice betrayal and hypocrisy they invariably only fool themselves, and at the same time betray themselves, not God. Again, God sees us before we see ourselves. "Be not deceived; God is not mocked: for whatsoever a man soweth, that he shall also reap" (Galatians 6:7).

Let's be entirely clear about it: there is no intent on the author's part to minimize the deaths and property losses that have occurred in the State of Texas due to recent devastating flooding. Human life is precious and the loss of any human life diminishes all of us, because what we invest in the lives of others comes back invariably into our own. Property can be rebuilt, restored, and replaced.

The State of Texas has requested and will receive Federal Emergency Management Assistance resources, and rightly so. Should there be arbitrariness in State decisions to apply for, request, and accept federal funds for man-made disasters? Of course, there are no questions about the necessity for assistance after, or concern for natural disasters (hurricanes, tornadoes, floods, earthquakes, and forest fires). Should State governments arbitrarily pick and choose what federal funds they will accept or reject for different types of disasters be they man-made or natural?

Is the lack of affordable healthcare for every Texan a man-made disaster? Simply put, health is wealth, and therefore ought to be a fundamental basic human right, especially since life is about swift transitions (an individual could be well today and bed-ridden tomorrow). Texas has the highest percentage of uninsured citizens (25%) of any State in these United States of America as well as the highest percent of uninsured children. Our children are our heritage and a living endowment for a brighter tomorrow. At the same time, Texas is among the wealthiest States in the Union, if not the wealthiest. With that being the case, why are so many Texan children and adults without adequate healthcare insurance and/or no coverage at all? This is a social fact that ought to be troubling to every Texan, especially Christian Texans.

Listed below are some Texas-sized man-made disaster healthcare facts:

- In 2015, twelve Bills were filed in the Texas Legislature proposing meaningful ways to close the healthcare insurance coverage gap in Texas, and not one bill passed. In the words of Congressman Alan Grayson (D-Florida), "die quickly."
- Over one million Texans are without health insurance coverage. The State of Texas ranks number one in the percentage of individuals without healthcare insurance, and number two in overall percentages.
- Texas ranks number one out of the sixteen States that have not adopted a healthcare insurance expansion plan.
- Since Texas has no healthcare coverage plan, over 6 billion in federal tax dollars were not received, and still remains in Washington. These federal dollars could create between 200-300 thousand new jobs. Closing the healthcare coverage gap would be a tremendous economic benefit in terms of meaningful employment opportunities for Texans.
- Healthcare insurance subsidies are only available to Texans who are above the poverty level. The individuals who need the subsidy the most

are not eligible because of the lack of a federal healthcare exchange system. Municipal and government entities have a moral obligation to their citizenry to at least provide adequate medical care if that resource is available. The Bible declares, "A little that a righteous man hath is better than the riches of many wicked" (Psalm 37:16). The impoverished citizens of Texas are denied their "little" because big State government has a distaste for the current administration and its policies.

These startling facts concerning healthcare coverage in Texas are not just about socio-political-economic issues, but spiritual and moral issues as well. That leads us to the God question and the Cain answer: "Where is Abel thy brother? And he said, Am I my brother's keeper?" (Genesis 4:9). Houstonians, as well as Texans from all over the State, have experienced a natural disaster of enormous proportions. At one point, Houston experienced twelve inches of rain in six hours, and at another time four inches of rain in one hour. God has said, "No more water, but the fire next time." The lack of healthcare for over one million Texans is a daily, disastrous man-made fire. As we well know, an individual can be healthy in the morning and become sick in the evening. They can be well in the morning and be on fire with fever that evening. Christian Texans need to warm up to loving and serving one another by making it known that they have accepted Jesus' clarion call to care for the "orphans and widows."

In closing, all Texans should embrace this supporting Scripture: "Verily I say unto you, Inasmuch as ye have done it unto one of the least of these my brethren, ye have done it unto me" (Matthew 25:40). Texas Christians need to file a class-action lawsuit on behalf of the least of them without affordable healthcare, because arbitrariness is a sin. Selah!

It's Midnight in America

30

Thirty-four years ago, President Ronald Reagan declared that it was morning in America. Without a doubt, America has been marching toward midnight for centuries because it has rightly been said that "a mind is a terrible thing to waste." Wasting human capital (minds) has finally taken its toll on American culture. America is in an institutional free-fall, especially in the Black community, because Black bodies are not in chains but some Black minds are still in bondage. Of course, Americans, in general, have forgotten where their help comes from. You may be asking yourself: What happened? But, more importantly, the real question is: What do you do when it is midnight? "If my people, which are called by my name, shall humble themselves, and pray and seek my face, and turn from their wicked ways; then will I hear from heaven, and will forgive their sin, and will heal their land" (II Chronicles 7:14). I must add as an answer to our present-day dilemma the experience of The New Testament writer, Paul, and his brother Silas. They found themselves unjustly imprisoned because of the mores of their era in what seemed to be an inescapable situation. They found the answer in turning to and praising God from whom all blessings flow (Acts 16:22-26).

Life is about commitment. God asked Adam the ultimate commitment question: Where art thou? In other words, where is your commitment and loyalty? Who are you standing with? Whom do you love more: Creator or creation? No matter how we frame the question, it is still about commitment because life is about commitment. These are difficult times in which we live, especially for the Black community. The economy grew at a robust 5% the final quarter of 2014, but high unemployment still exists in the Black community. The average American family cannot come up with $2,000 in thirty days even if their very existence depended upon it. The top two percent of individual wage earners in American society received roughly 90% of the increase in income wealth since the recovery of 2008. It is midnight in America. The private sector is building physical prisons at an alarming rate. Some pastoral and political leaders are erecting mental prisons at an even faster pace. How do we come from the other side of midnight? The New Testament writer Paul and Silas found the answer.

Paul and Silas were thrown in jail awaiting prosecution because they were servants of the Most High God. They prayed for deliverance and patiently waited upon God to deliver them because the battle is the Lord's (1 Samuel 17:47). Paul and Silas sanctified themselves in the TRUTH; God's Word is TRUTH. "Sanctify them through thy truth: thy word is truth" (John 17:17). Paul and Silas even while in prison asked GOD to "let their speech be always with grace, seasoned with salt, that ye may know how ye ought to answer every man" (Colossians 4:6). Paul and Silas found the answer and the road-map for both the spiritual prison business as well as the physical prison business. Their praying, praising, and patience created a spiritual conversion of a prison guard. Paul and Silas had been beaten and persecuted and their redemptive suffering caused God to produce a JAIL HOUSE ROCK of such a magnitude that even the jailer put up his sword and said: "What must I do in order to be saved?"

In modern times, we would say that the jailer's experience and that of all the prisoners could be equated with the infamous words of Elvis Presley: "I'm all shook-up." Prayer is internal self-introspection. Prayer is positive self-talk. Prayer is about bringing the "I" in each of us under submission to the "me" in each of us. The "I" in each of us is our ego. EGO is an acronym for Edge-God-Out. The "me" in each of us is the spiritual part of us that cries out to God: Lord, have mercy upon me a sinner. Of course, real prayer is using the words of God to talk to God. This is precisely why Dr. Martin Luther King, Jr., in the Black community's historic struggle for human and civil rights used the effective strategy of nonviolence combined with the prayers of the Black church nationwide.

Again, what do you do when you are in a dangerously bad situation? Believe me, the Black community is in a bad situation and has been in a bad situation since 1619. Black families are in spiritual shambles, Black churches are excessively materialistic and individualistically divisive, and too many Black leaders are self-serving. Too many Black colleges and universities (HBCUs) are degree-oriented rather than career-development oriented. Americans, especially Black Americans, should resolve to combat this modern day slavery through creative, spiritual living. We have witnessed the spiritual Star of Bethlehem. We should be willing to follow that spiritual Star to the Cross of Jesus Christ. But more importantly, because of the spiritual Star that is in the heart of our minds, we should be willing to love and serve one another. Therefore:

- We have seen the spiritual Star in all of its majestic glory. Jesus Christ is that Star that not only leads us to eternal life but eternal love.
- We have followed the spiritual Star that leads to the birthplace of our Lord and Savior, Jesus Christ, because the manger teaches all humanity this profound spiritual lesson about life: "For God so loved the world that he gave his only begotten Son, that whosoever believeth in him should not perish but have everlasting life" (John 3:16). The Ultimate Truth was born in a stable, wrapped in swaddling clothes, and gently laid in a manger. The Truth was not born in a high place, but in a lowly manger, because there was no room in the Inn for a Spiritual King.
- Many Christian believers have stood at the foot of the Cross of Jesus Christ and received

forgiveness and redemption from sin. But, more importantly, they have heard the voice of Jesus Christ saying, as He wrote in the sands of eternity: "He that is without sin cast the first stone."

Legalizing sin is not the answer. Seeking the face of God as Paul and Silas did is the answer. When it is midnight and your back is against the wall in a foreign land, internal self and community introspection is the only realistic course of action. Without a doubt, freedom is housed in self-initiatives, not in the slave master's house or within the prison walls. God has a divine purpose for Blacks being in America because Blacks are the conscience of America constitutionally whether good or bad. It is my earnest prayer that we have peace in America and express good will towards all. So be it!

31 | As a Man Thinketh, So Is He

The preamble to the Constitution and the Declaration of Independence are almost perfectly written spiritual documents. However, most individuals who have the privilege and social responsibility of interpreting these documents have been spiritually and morally flawed because they are heavily influenced by their socio-economic-religious backgrounds. This is why America has not been able to creatively live up to the moral tenets of the creed that "we hold these truths to be self-evident that all men are created equal." It is for this reason alone that America is not the melting-pot of the world community, which she proudly boasts to be. This is precisely why we have all of the lively social commentaries concerning Rachel Dolezal's self-identification.

This leads me to ask: Is race biology or sociology? Mankind has unequivocally declared that race is biology. However, the Bible states: "God that made the world and all things therein, seeing that he is Lord of heaven and earth, dwelleth not in temples made with hands; neither is worshipped with men's hands, as though he needed anything, seeing that he giveth to all life, and breath, and all things; and hath made of one blood all nations of men for to dwell on all the face of the earth, and hath determined the times before appointed, and the bounds of their habitation; that they should seek the Lord, if haply they might feel after him, and find him, though he be not far from every one of us: for in him we live, and move, and have our being; as certain also of your own poets have said, For we are also his offering" (Acts 17:24-28).

God hates racism. This writer believes that race is both biological and sociological, because as an individual thinketh, so is he. There are many Black Americans who defend establishment socio-economic-political policies that are designed to dehumanize their very existence as well as the existence of others who are physically like them. Life and death is not in skin color...except in a racist society.

There are many European Americans who defend the preamble to the Constitution as well as the Constitution, because they have effectively spiritually and morally "de-whitized" themselves. That is, these White Americans have effectively overcome their negative environmental socialization concerning racial identity.

Apparently, such is the case with Rachel Dolezal. The truth creates its own energy. A lie is fueled by borrowed energy, which requires agreement and needs help from many tellers. The truth is the truth whether an individual acknowledges it or not. Rachel Dolezal's self-identification as Black is real to her, which is a physical lie; but to her it is a truth in her heart and mind. According to her parents, Rachel has self-identified as Black since the age of five. This Scripture reflects that what Rachel Dolezal is attempting to accomplish is a state of internal peace given the historic nature of institutional racism: "And the peace of God, which passeth all understanding, shall keep your hearts and minds through Christ Jesus" (Philippians 4:7). Can there be any other reasonable explanation? If there is, my next question is: Why would an individual give up White privilege for Black cultural bondage in an institutionally racist society? It has often been said: "Once you go Black, you cannot go back." I do not know whether this statement is fact or fiction. Someone, please inform me.

What is it that has American society in such an uproar concerning the racial issue of a female self-identifying, who she thinks in her heart and mind that she is Black? I dare say that there are many Black Americans who are passing every day and twice on Sunday for European Americans. Rachel Dolezal was an unknown NAACP local chapter president, and now she is an international household name. The writer is not attempting to make this a sinless situation, but is it a crime given what Rachel was attempting to accomplish at the NAACP? In my opinion, the NAACP handled this situation with moral high-road dignity by declaring that being Black is not an occupational requirement. The objective of the NAACP is social justice, not the perpetuation of institutional racism.

There are only two social groups of individuals who are vocally bent out of shape about the racial overtones of the Rachel Dolezal situation. Everyone knows who they are and why they are so sensitive about the issue of individual freedom to cross the color line without so much fanfare. Who would dare believe that they are Black in a White body? Shame on you Rachel Dolezal for being spiritually free and so bold as to think outside of the box; stepping outside of the box is a no-no in American society, because racial identity is more powerful than issues of right versus wrong. The color-line is a powerful line of socio-economic demarcation. In my opinion, if an individual chooses to cross the color-line there is then another societal line that society judges that individual by: sanity and insanity. Society declares that there is a thin line between sanity and insanity, and also love and hate. Again, the Bible states: "For as he thinketh in his heart, so is he" (Proverbs 23:7).

What Greed and Inferiority Breed!

32

Murphy's Law declares that anything bad that can happen will happen. Of course, Murphy's Law is negative to its core. This writer does not embrace negativity, but expounds upon spiritual truth and facts. Such is the case with institutional-cultural inferiority because the case of mass murder in a historic Black affluent church in Charleston, South Carolina, is a classic example of cultural inferiority. I am not attempting to rub salt into the wounds of European Americans or American culture. Inferiority and insecurity do cause individuals to blame the victim for their own intellectual, spiritual, moral, and physical inadequacies.

The mass murder of Christians in Charleston, South Carolina, transcends Dylann Roof. I quote Dylann Roof because Dylann was a loser: "you are raping our women"; "taking over the country"; "you have to go." What is it that caused Dylann Roof and other like-minded European Americans to have polluted minds about race, and be willing to commit ungodly acts against minorities, especially Blacks? Is it because of low self-esteem (inferiority)?

This sense of cultural inferiority was transplanted by most European Americans, because they were looking for freedom but learned how to enslave. In the twenty-first century, Black Americans are seeking the exact same self-worth dignity-freedom that these immigrant European Americans were seeking in the sixteenth century. What a strange turn of events! European Americans came over on freedom ships; yet, Black Americans came to America on slave ships (mourning and groaning chained in their own human excrement). Without a doubt, in some instances, they were sold into slavery by other Black Africans, and marched to the coast in chains by Europeans and Arabs, then loaded aboard Jewish owned merchant slave ships headed to America. In this slave trade process, over six million Blacks died.

On arriving in America, Blacks were given a "pie in the sky" form of Christianity; that is, be a faithful slave to your master, and when you die you will be able to walk through the pearly gates on streets paved with gold, and flowing with milk and honey. In spite of this, some Blacks learned how to read, and investigated the truth of the master's declaration only to discover that he told a big European lie, and some had become corrupt, habitual liars laced with their own personal distorted facts. Europeans came seeking religious freedom, but learned how to teach and exploit Christianity to sell the "happy slave" concept. Thank God, for His everlasting word in a spiritually-morally dying world: "Heaven and earth shall pass away, but my words shall not pass away" (Matthew 24:35). More importantly, all Christians who are Christ-like know that "all Scripture is given by inspiration of God, and is profitable for doctrine, for reproof, for correction, for instruction in righteousness: that the man of God may be perfect, thoroughly furnished unto all good works" (1 Timothy 3:16-17).

Let's speak plainly about the issue of insecurity and inferiority. Dylann Roof stated that "Blacks are raping our women." Sex and racism is a real social conflict issue in American culture, especially to those who make it an issue because of their lack of security with the opposite sex. Even in war, sexuality is a real issue, because men will fight side by side and will even die for each other; yet they are not willing to share the same house of ill-repute (whorehouse) with each other because of race. What is the cause of this sexual-social dilemma? I propose that racial intolerance is at the root of America's sexual-social impasse.

Dylann Roof declared that he wanted to start a race war and take the country back. This writer can unequivocally declare that European Americans control and own America lock, stock, and barrel through laws that are established for European American privilege based upon the first line of defense (police constabularies). Police organizations are designed to protect European Americans and their property, and at the same time, keep minorities checkmated through intimidation and murder in the name of law and order. The purpose and culture of policing must be reformed so that we can have a more perfect union – that is, one nation under God. Who are we to take the country back from and for what purpose? Again, recent analysis confirms that European Americans own and socio-economically-politically control everything in this great nation, but God, even though some seek to play god. The surviving family members, Mother Emmanuel Church, and many God-fearing citizens of Charleston have already forgiven Dylann Roof. This is a powerful, universal testimony: "For there is one God, and one mediator between God and men, the man Christ Jesus; who gave himself a ransom for all to be testified in due time" (Timothy 2:5). As Americans, we need to learn the importance of "casting all your care upon him; for he careth for you" (1 Peter 5:7). These socio-spiritual-economic conditions must change, because Black lives matter, too!

Dylann Roof researched the history of Mother Emmanuel Church. Why? Is it because the history of Mother Emmanuel Church is glorious and spectacular in nature? This "Black" massacre was not an arbitrary act but initiated by research and design with the sole purpose to ignite a race-war. It was not mental illness that killed nine Black people; it was racial hatred.

Since the election of President Obama in 2008, many European American males, thirty and older, have completely gone ballistic and even wacko by attempting to destroy everything the Obama administration has attempted to accomplish. The objective is to destroy any vestige (legacy) of Obama ever being president or the leader of the free-world. Shame, shame because this has had a negative impact on American culture and the notion of the melting-pot. Of course, the international community sees America for what she truly is: A nation that is still divided by race and ethnicity!

This state of affairs has truly affected the image that the millennial generation has transcended the color-line. Not so fast, news media personalities; racism is alive and well. But, after almost four hundred years, racism should be buried in its grave. And, no one should be given the privilege of saying these things take time. Are we to wait another four hundred years for things to change? If this writer did not know better one would be tempted to believe that we are pre-era (1964) Civil Rights Act and 1965 Voting Rights Act. Selah!

Institutional Racism Versus the Peacemaker

33

It has rightly been said: "the killer (Dylann Roof) is in a South Carolina jail, but the real killers are walking around free." Racial hatred killed Pastor Pinckney and eight other Christian believers in Mother Emmanuel Church. Who are the individuals (cultural forces) that taught Dylann Roof to hate other individuals simply because God made their skin color different? Without a doubt, institutional racism is still alive and well. Individuals who have a problem with skin-color invariably have a God-problem (spiritual problem). Let's be perfectly clear about one thing: No individual makes himself/herself. God makes us all. He has declared that I knew you before you were conceived.

209

No individual can control another person's spiritual ignorance of God. Was Dylann Roof born into American society as a child of predilection or an expression of divine love (as a child of God)? Maybe Dylann's problem is revealed to us in the following idiom: "Apples do not fall too far from the tree."

Symbols motivate human behavior; however, the Confederate Flag did not teach Dylann Roof to hate, even though it is a symbol of hatred. Without a doubt, the Confederate Flag is only a symbol of socio-spiritual-injustice (racial-hatred). Personally, I do not worship flags, but I do worship a living God who loves all individuals in spite of skin color, because God hates racism. The individuals who died fighting under the Confederate Flag died for an unjust cause. Even though, possessing slaves at one time in American history was legal and not a crime because slaves were considered the property of White males, their inhumane treatment made it morally illegal. White women were also treated as property. Far more important, succeeding from the Federal Union was an act of treason. All of the individuals who fought and died under the Confederate battle Flag were traitors to the United States of America.

What then is the connection between the

Confederate Flag proudly being displayed on social media by Dylann Roof and his statement: "You are raping our women?" Rape is a horrific crime, which must not be tolerated by any committed. White females are being raped on college campuses by White males at an alarming rate. Are White females still the property of White males? Based upon the Confederate doctrine, is hatred in the DNA of White southerners? There are many who say you can take down the Confederate Flag, but you cannot change the heart (spiritual-mind-set), "For as he thinketh in his heart, so is he" (Proverbs 23:7).

The Confederate Flag represents White supremacy even though some Whites desire revisionist history. Two months after the election of President Lincoln, South Carolina seceded from the Union; the first shot in the Civil War was fired at Fort Sumter, South Carolina. The Southern States fighting for slavery presented an international image problem, and, therefore, Confederate image-makers came up with the concept of States-Rights. Hence, if the Confederate Flag is simply American history as some declare, then maybe the most historically appropriate place for the Confederate Flag is in museums, not on State Capitol grounds. Maybe there is such an animal as "Lost Cause Mythology."

When will it be spiritually-morally acceptable to be Black in America, especially since same-sex marriage is now legal? To be sure, if the majority of whites were against White supremacy (privilege), then institutional racism would not exist. We all know that silence is consent. America involved itself in a world war against other European Whites who believed that some whites were not white enough (Nazism). Will America ever spiritually rid its culture of the spiritual forces of institutional racism? Again, I ask: When will it be legally and spiritually acceptable to be Black in America? The only allowable refuge blacks have in America is the Christian church (the house of God) and prison (the house of the devil).

America has a God (spiritual) problem: God-centered Christianity versus culture-centered Christianity. God made us all. Why, then, can't we worship God together? Why can't we stop burning Black churches and denying Blacks equal opportunity and relishing in White privilege? This problem is precisely why America has not been able to transcend the color-line and become the idealized melting-pot of the world community. It is for this reason alone (White privilege) that Blacks and Whites do not worship God together in the same sanctuary. Skin color is not God. God is God all by Himself. For it is written, "Thou shalt have no other gods before me" (Exodus 20:3). "If a man say, I love God, and hateth his brother, he is a liar: for he that loveth not his brother whom he hath seen, how can he love God whom he hath not seen" (1 John 4:20).

The pastor, State-Senator Pinckney, was a peacemaker and a man of deep spiritual faith. In his everyday living, he lived the concept of the church without walls (Great Commission). Senator Pinckney was known for bridging communication gulfs and pulling down immoral walls of mistrust and political confusion among his Senate colleagues. Pastor Pinckney was highly respected as a pastoral leader and beloved as a statesman, not a politician. I sincerely believe that Pastor Pinckney's soul is in the care of Almighty God, "because he set his affection on things above, not on things on the earth" (Colossians 3:2). Pastor Pinckney's faith was based on decisions and not on emotional feelings.

Every individual clearly expresses God's love when they "do the right thing" and live by Biblical principles and precepts. Of course, if an individual does not know what the right thing is, then clearly he/she has a real problem. Is chattel slavery dead? Is conflict-confusion what is meant by the Southern slogan, "the

South will rise again"?

Individuals can only do the right thing when they are able to deal effectively with self-introspection and self-examination based upon Biblical principles and precepts. The Black church is the heart and soul of the Black experience in America. President Obama,in his home-going celebration of Pastor Pinckney's life, captured the moment in both his eulogy and rendition of "Amazing Grace," because it is God's grace and mercy that profoundly expresses God's love for us. We all know that "There is a way which seemeth right unto a man; but the end thereof are the ways of death" (Proverbs 14:12). Dylann Roof was victimized by Confederate culture because the wages of sin is death, and the gift of God is eternal life. We give no place to the devil. Those nine Christians of Mother Emmanuel Church are in heaven with God; because the gift of God is eternal life! Selah.

Free-Enterprise Based Upon Greed Is Long-Suffering

34

Greed produces individual as well as societal suffering. The bottom-line in the American free-enterprise system is what Wall Street wants and what Wall Street gets, because Wall Street and capitalism are too big to fail. But, on the other hand, the system is designed for corporation successes and individual failures, that is, blame the victims for their own economic failures. Most individuals, especially minorities, play into the hands of the capitalist image-makers to maintain social class privilege. Of course, "The man that wandereth out of the way of understanding shall remain in the congregation of the dead" (Proverbs 21:16).

When is enough, enough? The wealth of American Capitalists do not go toward building moral character, fostering economic justice, and educational opportunities for American families, but instead is invested and hidden in foreign countries, especially foreign banks. The elite capitalists do not want to even pay their fair share of taxes to improve the socio-spiritual-economic stability of a dying and decadent American society (reference Warren Buffet). The economic greed of vulgar capitalists is primarily oriented toward pleasure-seeking opportunities rather than societal socio-spiritual development (societal stability). Righteousness exalts a nation and evil is a reproach to God. "But she that liveth in pleasure is dead while she liveth" (1 Timothy 4:6). This Scripture is applicable to all extravagant pleasure seekers, especially men, because they turn to each other for pleasure. My parents taught me that "an idle mind and pleasure seeking are the devil's workshop." Without a doubt, greed is the primary cause of an idle mind and invariably creates the devil's playground, because greed creates inordinate affection. "Mortify therefore your members which are upon the earth; fornication, uncleanness, inordinate affection, evil concupiscence, and covetousness, which is idolatry: for which things' sake the wrath of God cometh on the children of the disobedience" (Colossians 3:5).

It takes an entire American society to become a righteous example for other nations. If America exemplified national and international moral character (i.e., spiritually lived up to its own Constitution) rather than that of the characterization of the "ugly American," then we might have the moral respect of the community of nations as an honest broker (peacemaker). If living up to the spiritual tenets of the Constitution has been almost impossible for us at this time, attempting to spread democracy abroad makes us hypocrites. Of course, America can influence any nation-state with a "carrot and a stick" for a short while to go along to get along, that is, do America's national bidding. Can America make peace in foreign countries when America does not have economic justice and moral criminal justice for all Americans?

The American economic system is built upon slave labor. At one time, Capitalism was built upon chattel slave labor. In the twenty-first century, Capitalism is built upon illegal immigrant slave labor. Either way, it is corporate welfare for Capitalists and bread without butter welfare for the poor. The trickle-down economics approach has taken American society to the other side of midnight (societal-economic inequality), because the rich are getting richer, and, by economic design, the poor make the rich, rich. Economic inequality is directly linked to an individual's ability to obtain a quality education, especially a college education. How do we as a society build wealth? By investing in people rather than Investing in things. Investing in things is a disastrous pathway for a democratic society. Things do not think and create, but are created by thinkers (human beings). This is precisely why income inequality is such a serious socio-economic problem. By and large, the rich do not invest proportionally in human development, spiritual-moral development, and educational institutions. But, on the other hand, the rich spend vulgar sums of money on jet-carriers, yachts, castles, islands, and servants, all designed to hide their vulgarity and opulent life styles of pleasure-seeking, because four hundred individuals in America have more wealth than one-half the American population. Too much wealth is concentrated in the hands of the top one-percent of Americans.

The middle-class is being squeezed off the socio-economic playing field, and, without a viable middle-class, the American economic system cannot sustain itself. The rich and the super-rich want the middle-class to be similar to them in lifestyle, but not the same in structural-value orientation. Moreover, the middle class want the working-class to mimic their lifestyle, but not have the same structural-value orientation.

The trickle-down economic approach to nation building has created a wealth gap of monumental proportions, because the trickle-down economic effect has had a monumental negative impact on the quality of American social life. America needs to invest in the educational development of our children, rebuild its infrastructure, diminish the influence of money in politics, make our transportation systems safer, and above all, reject the spiritual decadence of so-called same-sex marriage.

America needs to clearly understand that "There is no wisdom nor understanding nor counsel against the Lord" (Proverbs 21:30). But, more importantly, "The man that wandereth out of the way of understanding shall remain in the congregation of the dead" (Proverbs 21: 16). To be sure, a zombie is a card carrying member of the walking dead club, because he/she is walking around creating motion and chaos without spiritual understanding and purpose, that is, doing the devil's business, not God's business. Selah!

35 | Has American Society Devolved Into a Culture of Death?

"Then said Jesus unto him, Put up again thy sword into his place: for all they that take the sword shall perish with the sword" (Matthew 26:52). In the twenty-first century the sword is the gun. The greedy are making money off of their acronym GOD: (G) guns, (O) oil, and (D) drugs, including war. The God of our salvation is not pleased, because "God judge the righteous and is angry with the wicked every day" (Psalm 7:11). Because of guns, our children are being slaughtered in public schools, individuals are being mass-slaughtered in entertainment venues,

Christian parishioners are being slaughtered in church houses, unarmed military recruiting officers are being slaughtered in recruitment centers, and police officers are killing unarmed citizens as though it is a badge of honor. Of course, all spiritual-moral-minded individuals know "That the house of the wicked shall be overthrown: but the tabernacle of the upright shall flourish" (Proverbs 14:11).

There is a misinterpretation of the Second Amendment that is distorting the minds, moral character, and spiritual understanding of American citizens. Life and death are in the hands of God, not in the hands of American citizens who possess over three hundred million guns. The Bible declares that life and death are in the tongue. "Be not deceived: evil communications corrupt good manners. Awake to righteousness, and sin not; for some have not the knowledge of God: I speak this to your shame" (1 Corinthians 14:33-34). Did the writers of the Second Amendment intend that every American citizen carry a gun "to and fro," "everywhere they go," that is, become his own militia? In the early days of America's existence this was an acceptable practice, because there was neither an organized militia nor a police constabulary to protect individual citizens from Native Americans as well as from the British army, therefore, each individual was required to protect himself from demise.

Jesus declared that He came that individuals might have life and have life more abundantly. Jesus Christ suffered, died, shed His precious blood, and rose from the dead so that we as Christians might come to know: "Verily, verily I say unto you, He that heareth my word, and believeth on him that sent me, hath everlasting life, and shall not come into condemnation; but is passed from death unto life" (John 5:24). Guns and more guns are not the answer to moral-value conflicts between individuals in a civilized society. It seems as though it takes death to move Americans to do the right thing, not an expression of life and life more abundantly.

When one thinks about it, guns and hate symbols do not mix, especially since symbols motivate behavior. This combination produces explosive negative emotions with physical negative results, because it is like pouring gasoline on a fire that is already burning out of control. To be sure, there is a certain level of spiritual and intellectual ignorance present in every individual, because there is such a thing as an educated fool, meaning: an individual can be a graduate of the most prestigious "hallowed-halls-ofesteemed-academia" and yet is an educated fool. Individuals must have a spiritual-moral compass with eyes fixed on the prize (salvation). There is also such a thing as those who are spiritually dead to the Word of God as recorded in Holy Scriptures. "For I say, through the grace given unto me, to every man that is among you, not to think of himself more highly than he ought to think; but to think soberly, according as God hath dealt to every man the measure of faith" (Romans 12:3). Too many Americans have become card-carrying members in the army of the spiritually dead, preaching hatred and bigotry yet still attempting to fill the everlasting void in their empty souls. The greedy invariably become the needy.

"And this is life eternal, that they might know thee the only true God, and Jesus Christ, whom thou hast sent" (John 17:3). Jesus did not come to teach individuals how to die, but how they should live, and above all, how to love and serve one another.

Why haven't Blacks taken up arms against European Americans given the level of violence and dehumanization of Black Americans? In this writer's mind, it is not because Blacks fear Europeans or anyone else on planet earth, but because we fear the wrath and judgment of Almighty God. Fear of the

Lord is wisdom, because Blacks know that there is safety in the Lord. So that there is no misunderstanding, even among Blacks, there are some dysfunctional spiritual and moral exceptions to the spiritual and moral will of God.

"So then every one of us shall give account of himself to God" (Romans 14: 12). God's Word is so high that you cannot go over it. God's Word is so low that you can't get under it. God's Word is so wide that you can't go around it. You must go through God's sanctified word of truth by way of faith to get through it. Faith comes by hearing and hearing by the Word of God. "Sanctify them through thy truth: thy word is truth" (John 17:17). "But without faith it is impossible to please him: for he that cometh to God must believe that he is, and that he is a rewarder of them that diligently seek him" (Hebrews 11:6). So be it!

 # Conclusion

American society is at a socio-spiritual-economic crossroads. Which way, America: national unity or national chaos? America is victimized by a religious and political leadership mentality that is overly materialistic, self-serving, and obsolete. Where there is spiritual leadership ignorance, the people perish. Politics should be about universal moral values and economic justice for all, not political party identification. The problem is not the Republican Party and the solution is not the Democratic Party. Seemingly, the problem is a lack of spiritual and moral respect for each other as children of God as well as as American citizens. To be sure, too many Americans have turned inward (i.e., become self-serving), building bigger barns and only preparing for greater material profits.

Rugged individualistic materialism has enslaved the very soul of American society. Individualism is and has always been the very soul of the divide and conquer tactic. This observation was profoundly stated by President Abraham Lincoln: "A house divided against itself cannot stand." Wake-up, everybody, before the moral walls tumble down and God pulls the final curtain down. What time is it? It's wake-up time!

America is being destroyed internally because of spiritual immorality and socio-political-economic greed. External forces will not be the cause of America's demise, but self-serving greed is the culprit.

In this collection of essays, the author has creatively sought to address the pressing spiritual, moral, and socio-political-economic issues plaguing America's basic primary institutions: family, church, and educational. The question is: What kind of America do we want? There are two kinds of individuals in this world: givers and takers. The issue of greed is breeding a large, self-serving class of takers. Giving is for the giver, not the receiver.

Social scientists, especially sociologists, have a two-fold moral charge:

- The first charge is to help White America learn to live up to the discipline of their own conscience and the spiritual words as recorded and agreed to in the Preamble to the U.S. Constitution: "We hold these truths to be self-evident that all men are created equal, that they are endowed by their Creator with certain inalienable rights, and among these are life, liberty and the pursuit of happiness."
- The next charge is similar in nature to the first one. Social scientists must help minorities, especially blacks, understand the nature of cause and effect; that is, the consequences of their own behavior concerning their own socio-economic plight. Without a doubt, white behavior has been notoriously bad over the past three hundred and ninety-three years, and some whites had set seemingly inerasable bad examples. This is why we still have covert institutional racism in the twenty-first century. We do not have racism by law, but racism still exists in individual mindsets and in institutional

power resources. Race matters and race still plays a covert role in American society even though the physical, overt manifestations of racism are far less pronounced.

No living human being can do more for an individual than that individual can do for himself or herself. The nature of our social problems are both spiritual as well as sociological. Lack of economic power (resources) in American society is not the problem. Spiritual understanding and spiritual-moral will are the problems, which in turn, expresses itself in the lack of spiritual knowledge, lack of economic organization, and lack of societal unity.

First, American family life must be revamped spiritually. Families have a moral duty to do a much better job of disciplining their children. To honor your mother and father is a moral obligation (Exodus 20:12). We have left two generations of children behind because of bad attitudes. Simply put, bad attitudes place bricks on prison walls. Additionally, bad attitudes have placed a communication barrier between children and their families. The results of this has been children using gangs as surrogate family structures. Another monumental problem is children having children. And last, our children using street drugs is a recipe for sleepwalking through life and all manner of dysfunction.

Christian churches must be realigned because too many pastoral leaders have replaced the life and teachings of Jesus Christ as the foundation of the church with personality "isms and schisms." Many are called, but few are chosen of God because God's pastors know God's voice and exemplify Christ-like character in the way they love and serve. Worldly preachers, rather than feeding God's sheep as under-shepherds to the Good Shepherd (Jesus Christ), are eating the sheep and sometimes even breeding the sheep. There is a difference between a pastor and a preacher (Ephesians 4:11). As a result, America is becoming less religious (spiritual) and more secular (humanist).

The church should be leading the moral charge for the responsibility of parents to morally discipline children in the home and for public schools to provide a quality education. Instead, too many pastoral leaders are fostering personal gain rather than community development. The objective seems to be to build a mega-church to get more individuals in the pews, to get more financial gain from the collection plate, to build an even larger church. The question is, why? Is it to strengthen families one by one? I do not think so. Is it to educate our children one by one? I do not think so. Is it to help the widows and orphans in local communities one by one? I do not think so. Is it to build residential (single family) homes one by one? I do not think so! If these were the spiritual and moral plans of action, I would be the first to say glory to God in the highest and peace on earth toward all men. The spiritual intent should not be just to blame, but to reclaim.

American society has lost its way and is wandering in the wilderness of spiritual ignorance of God and His intent, because too many Christian pastors have led the church away from its foundation. As a result, we have a group of individuals called millennials who have been materialized rather than spiritualized. Millennials do not know God and do not attend church. This is one of the many and varied reasons why Christianity is on the decline in American society. Even older Americans are disavowing organized religion. Baby-boomers identify their religion as "none" (seventeen percent), which makes the "nones" the fastest growing religion in American society.

Educators at every level must teach our students that

education is a process of learning how to think critically and to analyze. That is a choice between God's blessings and the devil's curse. In the final analysis, teachers must present to students the choice between America's blessings and America's curse. Teaching is about the discovery of truth and making comparative analyzes. It is not about how intellectually brilliant teachers think they are, but how boldly they can tell the truth, and how faithfully they can love and serve students.

Teachers and professors at every educational level must make a concerted professional effort to ensure that America gets it right in the twenty-first century. Reprogramming someone's mindset is not an easy task. In our educational institutions, we must begin to teach students what is spiritually and morally right, not what is popular. This approach to teaching and learning will foster a renaissance of the human spirit in American culture. Teachers and professors have a moral duty to provide a holistic approach to education and learning, and presently, it does not exist. Teachers and educators must find creative ways to help students overcome negative instincts because God is not Santa Claus; creative living requires self-sacrifice; that is, teachers and professors must find creative ways to help students not become their own worst enemy.

The author is a more loving, understanding, and spiritually-minded individual because of the learning experience involved in writing this book. I earnestly hope that those who read this book will realize that reading is developmental.

www.ingramcontent.com/pod-product-compliance
Lightning Source LLC
Chambersburg PA
CBHW071339280526
45787CB00001B/144